PUBLISHED FOR THE MALONE SOCIETY BY
OXFORD UNIVERSITY PRESS

GREAT CLARENDON STREET, OXFORD OX2 6DP

Oxford New York
Athens Auckland Bangkok Bogota Bombay Buenos Aires
Calcutta Cape Town Dar es Salaam Delhi Florence Hong Kong Istanbul
Karachi Kuala Lumpur Madras Madrid Melbourne Mexico City
Nairobi Paris Singapore Taipei Tokyo Toronto Warsaw

and associated companies in
Berlin Ibadan

ISBN 0 19 729038 8

Printed by BAS Printers Limited, Over Wallop, Hampshire

THE COUNTRY CAPTAIN
BY
WILLIAM CAVENDISH,
EARL OF NEWCASTLE

THE MALONE SOCIETY
REPRINTS, VOL. 162
1999

This edition of *The Country Captain* by William Cavendish, Earl of Newcastle, has been prepared by Anthony Johnson, revised by H. R. Woudhuysen, and checked by Katherine Duncan-Jones and Richard Proudfoot.

The Society is grateful to the British Library for permission to edit the text and reproduce pages from its manuscript, Harl. MS 7650.

November 1998 H. R. Woudhuysen

CONTENTS

Introduction vii

THE MANUSCRIPT: PROVENANCE vii
PAPER AND WATERMARKS ix
HANDS, SCRIBES, AND SUBSTANTIVE CHANGES xii
BRACKETING xvii
DATING xx
ATTRIBUTION AND AUTHORSHIP xxiii
EDITORIAL CONVENTIONS xxviii
LIST OF CHARACTERS xxxiii

Plates 1–4 xxxv–xxxviii

Text 1

INTRODUCTION

The Country Captain has usually been ascribed to William Cavendish (1592–1676), Earl and subsequently first Duke of Newcastle. It exists in two main primary forms: an untitled manuscript (British Library, Harley MS 7650), and an edition printed at The Hague in 1649 and reissued in London during the same year. The Hague edition, in which authorship was unattributed, was not published there; the sheets were brought to London where it was published by Humphrey Moseley with *The Variety*, as two plays by a nobleman. Both appeared under a general title-page, although each also had a separate title-page. The printed versions of the play differ slightly from the manuscript, but for his issue Moseley was able to supply a prologue and an epilogue, as well as a passage at the beginning of the fourth act. A modern edition of the play, prepared from the manuscript by A. H. Bullen under the title *Captain Underwit, A Comedy*, was printed at London in 1883 in the second volume of *A Collection of Old English Plays*. Bullen, initially unaware of the existence of the 1649 version, thought he had recovered a lost work by James Shirley, to whom he attributed the play. It is in this form—supplemented by the Benjamin Blom reissue of Bullen's work in 1964—that *The Country Captain* has found its main avenue of transmission to a twentieth-century audience.[1]

The Manuscript: Provenance

The unique manuscript of *The Country Captain*—in a nineteenth-century binding stamped with the Harleian crest—is in the British Library. Neither the British Library catalogues, nor W. W. Greg—who described Harley MS 7650 in 1931—provide any clear indication about its provenance before it entered the holdings of the British Museum, although palaeographical evidence shows it to date from the middle of the seventeenth century and to

[1] The full title of The Hague edition of the play is 'THE|COVNTRY CAPTAINE|A|COMOEDYE|LATELY PRESENTED|By his Majesties Servants|at the Blackfryers.|[lace ornament]|IN s'Grave van Haghe.|Printed by Samuell Broun English|Bookeseller at the Signe of the English|Printing house in the Achterome.|Anno 1649.' (hereafter referred to as *The Country Captaine*). In the English issue, this is bound with its companion play, and both are subsumed under the more general title of 'The Country|CAPTAINE,|And the|VARIETIE,|Two|COMEDIES,|Written by a Person|of *HONOR*. || Lately presented by His|*MAJESTIES* Servants, at|the *Black-Fryers*. || *LONDON*,|Printed for *Hum*: *Robinson* at the *Three-*|*Pidgeons,* and *Hum*: *Moseley* at the|*Princes Armes* in St. *Pauls* Church-|yard. 1649.'; W. W. Greg, *A Bibliography of the English Printed Drama to the Restoration*, 4 vols. (London, 1939–59), nos. 681, 692, iii. 1031–2.

The Victorian edition is entitled *Captain Underwit, A Comedy*, ed. A. H. Bullen, *A Collection of Old English Plays*, 4 vols. (London, 1882–5, rpt. New York, 1964), ii. 315–416 (hereafter referred to as *Captain Underwit*).

A valuable edition of the play was prepared by Marie Virginia Lavis as 'An Edition of *The Country Captaine* ("Captain Underwit") from B. M. Harleian MS. 7650 and the Edition of 1649' as an unpublished University of London MA in 1963 (hereafter referred to as 'Lavis').

include autograph revisions by William Cavendish.[2] The designation '5001' on the flyleaf (Fol. iia), however, does indicate the manuscript was acquired by the Trustees of the British Museum between 1756 and 1782, and was transferred to the Harleian collection after that time.

The previous item in Samuel Ayscough's catalogue of manuscripts from this period, Additional MS 5000, like the former Additional MS 5001, was also moved to the Harleian collection and became Harley MS 7649.[3] That folio manuscript contains two pieces bound together: a 'Divination with Lilly the Astrologer who should be Author of a second Advice to A Painter' (Fols. 1–5), and 'A Poem on The Recovery of the Lady Henrietta Hollis From the Small Pox. Humbly Dedicated to his Grace The Duke of Newcastle By his most Obedient Servant, Susanna Centlivre' (Fols. 6–10).[4]

Under normal circumstances, of course, there is no particular reason why adjacent entries in the catalogue of a manuscript collection should be related to each other. But in this case, the two manuscripts may share an earlier provenance. In his catalogue, Ayscough numbered the entries for this phase in the history of the Additional series in order of acquisition, so that it is not unlikely that the former Additional MSS 5000 and 5001 reached him at about the same time. Such a supposition is reinforced by the fact that the title-leaves of the 'Divination' and the Centlivre poem (Fols. 1a and 6a) and the fly-leaf of *The Country Captain* (Fol. iia) have numbers in Ayscough's hand and have been corrected in the same ink (presumably at the same sitting): the earlier designations '4500' and '4501' have been struck out and replaced by '5000' and '5001' respectively.[5] Since *The Country Captain* contains manuscript corrections in the Earl of Newcastle's hand and Centlivre's poem is dedicated to Thomas Pelham-Holles (1693–1768), Duke of Newcastle, who had married Henrietta, daughter of the second Earl of Godolphin, in 1717, the two manuscripts can be associated with the Dukes of Newcastle: William Cavendish's son Henry (1630–91), the second Duke of Newcastle, was the father of Lady Margaret Cavendish who married John Holles (1662–1711), Duke of Newcastle; he left his fortune to his nephew Thomas Pelham-Holles. His daughter, Henrietta, married Edward Harley. Furthermore, their simultaneous treatment by Ayscough suggests they could have travelled together from an earlier source; this is worth pursuing since it might offer a plausible clue as to the previous history of Harley MS 7650. The provenance of the Centlivre part of Additional MS 5000 is

[2] See W. W. Greg, *Dramatic Documents from the Elizabethan Playhouses*, 2 vols. (Oxford, 1931), i. 362–3. The British Library *Catalogue of Additions to the Manuscripts 1756–1782: Additional Manuscripts 4101–5017* (London, 1977), p. 301, merely reports that the manuscript has been renumbered; no earlier provenance is recorded for it in Cyril Ernest Wright, *Fontes Harleiani: A Study of the Sources of the Harleian Collection of Manuscripts Preserved in the Department of Manuscripts in the British Museum* (London, 1972), p. 475.

[3] BL, Add. MS 5015, Fol. 120a, where MS Harley 7650 is described as 'A Play, no Name'. For Ayscough, see also the British Library *Catalogue of Additions 1756–1782*, p. v.

[4] The first piece is by Christopher Wase and dates from 1666–7, see *Poems on Affairs of State*, ed. George deF. Lord *et al.*, 7 vols. (New Haven, Conn., and London, 1963–75), i. 54–66.

[5] The former Additional MSS 4500–1 formed part of the ninety-four volumes of transcripts made by Thomas Madox (1666–1727), which were presented to the British Museum by his widow Catherine in 1756.

known: on Fol. 6a, it has 'Welbeck' written in the hand of Humfrey Wanley, librarian to Robert Harley and to his son Edward. Initially, therefore, it had been part of the Cavendish–Holles Library at Welbeck Abbey, Nottinghamshire, the seat of the Dukes of Newcastle until 1716. From 1718 onwards, the Library was moved to Robert Harley's Dover Street House in London for absorption into his collection. As C. E. Wright observed, only a 'handful' of the Cavendish–Holles manuscripts can be positively identified; but it would be by no means unlikely that Additional MS 5001 should have been among the unidentified items. If this is correct, it would have remained in the Library at Welbeck after the death of the first Duke of Newcastle in 1676, and accompanied Additional MS 5000 into the Harleian collection in the earlier years of the eighteenth century. Edward Harley was, after all, married to Lady Henrietta Holles and it was only after the death of her mother, the Duchess of Newcastle, on 24 December 1716, that the Holles library was moved from Welbeck.[6] In this context, as P. L. Heyworth has noted, 'Harley kept all the manuscripts and such printed books as he wanted', and the text of *The Country Captain* may well have been among them.[7] However, in the absence of hard evidence either way, such speculations as to the provenance of Harley MS 7650 must remain tentative.

Paper and Watermarks

The main part of Harley MS 7650 was originally written on twenty-one gatherings of four leaves, to form a quarto volume of eighty-four leaves, each measuring approximately 150 mm × 198 mm. The loss of parts of letters in the outer margins (for example, on Fols. 2a, 6a, 10a, 13a, and 19a and b) shows that the manuscript has been trimmed at some point: the outer edges of its leaves are not gilded. Inserted on a stub in the centre of the final gathering is a single larger sheet. It is 264 mm high, but has been cut unevenly and repaired with some loss of text to the outer margin, so that it now measures approximately 190 mm across its top and 196 mm across its foot: the foot and right-hand side of its outer edges have been folded in to fit the rest of the manuscript's smaller format. Uniquely in the manuscript, the lower edge of the leaf has been gilded.

The leaves of the manuscript's first gathering were blank until Ayscough wrote on the second leaf the manuscript's earlier Additional numbers, to which Frederic Madden added an explanatory note with the new Harleian number. The text and foliation (which is contemporary) begin on the second gathering: the insert (Fol. 78+), which was not foliated by the main scribe

[6] See Wright, *Fontes Harleiani*, pp. 350, 475; *The Diary of Humfrey Wanley 1715–1726*, ed. C. E. Wright and Ruth C. Wright, 2 vols. (London, 1966), i. xl–xlii.

[7] *Letters of Humfrey Wanley: Palaeographer, Anglo-Saxonist, Librarian, 1672–1726*, ed. P. L. Heyworth (Oxford, 1989), p. 386, n. 2. One of the texts gathered in this way is Harley MS 4955, the celebrated 'Newcastle' Manuscript, containing poems by Donne, Jonson, and others, in the hand of John Rolleston, Newcastle's scribe, see *The Diary of Humfrey Wanley*, i. xlii. For the bulk of the surplus books subsequently sold as the property of the first three Dukes of Newcastle, see *Bibliotheca Nobilissimi Principis Johannis Ducis de Novo-Castro, etc., being a large collection of books contained in the libraries of William and Henry Cavendish, and John Hollis, late Dukes of Newcastle . . . which will be sold by Nath. Noel, 2nd March 1718–19* (London, 1719).

but bears the deleted number 6 in ink (inverted in its top-right corner), falls between the folios marked 78 and 79. On Fol. 29a, towards the right-hand side of the lower margin, the scribe has written the number 4 (the descender has been trimmed); the number 6 (with the lower part of the bowl trimmed) occurs in the same position on Fol. 37a. These numbers coincide with the beginning of the manuscript's eighth and tenth gatherings: their relationship to its present construction is not clear.

The manuscript's leaves are crossed by horizontal chain-lines approximately 28 mm apart (the addition, by vertical chain-lines also approximately 28 mm apart), but more significantly, the manuscript has a series of watermarks which show it was written on two main stocks of paper. The watermarks straddle the leaves of the gatherings, appearing in most instances on the outer folios (1 and 4) and the inner folios (2 and 3) as matching pairs. The tightness of the manuscript's binding adds to the difficulty of identifying the watermarks.

In the first part of the manuscript the watermark consists of a fool's cap from which a trefoil is suspended; associated with this are the initials 'E D' and what may be the letter 'L'. The watermarks of this first stock of paper appear regularly throughout gatherings three to seven (Fols. 5–24). The second part of the manuscript has a watermark of a banner with two pennants meeting at the middle, flying from a staff, with a countermark consisting of the initials 'b' and 'V' suspended from a trefoil and joined by a bar. These watermarks of the second stock appear regularly throughout gatherings eight to twenty (Fols. 25–76). The first, almost entirely blank, gathering has the banner and staff of the second stock at its centre (Fols. ii–iii). The gathering's fourth leaf is unwatermarked, as is the first, which is almost certainly from a more modern stock of paper and is probably conjunct with the manuscript's last leaf (Fol. 80). The watermarks of the second gathering show some disturbance: the central leaves (Fols. 2 and 3) have the fool's cap and trefoil, and although the first leaf has the trefoil, the fourth is unwatermarked. In the manuscript's final gathering (Fols. 78–9) the central leaves are both unwatermarked; its first leaf has the staff—the final leaf, which does not bear contemporary foliation, belongs to a different stock of paper.

The evidence that the watermarks themselves provide as to the age and provenance of the paper is suggestive but inconclusive. The banner and the staff of the second stock of paper, bear some resemblance to Heawood 1371.[8] The association of the banner and staff with the 'b–V' trefoil motif does not appear in the literature on the subject. In isolation, the configuration of trefoil and monogram is similar to that in Heawood 997 (from Giuseppe Rosaccio's edition of Ptolemy (Venice, 1598)) although there it is associated with a crown; and nothing resembling it is to be found in Briquet's or Churchill's volumes, which take their examples, in the main, from western-European sources.[9] Mošin, on the other hand, working largely with papers from Bel-

[8] Edward Heawood, *Watermarks Mainly of the 17th and 18th Centuries* (Hilversum, 1950); the watermark is tentatively dated '1637', although its place of origin is not supplied.

[9] C. M. Briquet, *Les Filigranes*, ed. A. Stevenson, 4 vols. (Amsterdam, 1968). W. A. Churchill, *Watermarks in Paper* (Amsterdam, 1935), is similarly unforthcoming with respect to this motif.

grade and its environs, cites a number of closer south-east European examples—some dating from as late as 1647—although the implications of such a finding probably relate more to the spread of Italian paper bearing the banner motif than they do to *The Country Captain*.[10]

Nearer home, however, among the Portland papers housed in the Hallward Library at Nottingham University, are a number of Newcastle papers which are more closely comparable to the configuration of banner, staff, and 'b–V' trefoil motif found within Harley MS 7650. In Portland MS Pw V 26, for instance, the banner motif may be found on Fols. 79–80, which bear the text of Newcastle's poems, 'Loue's Epitaph' (Fol. 79a) and 'Loue's Resurrection' (Fols. 79a–80a) in the hand of Newcastle's secretary John Rolleston. The leaves make up a single folded sheet, each folio measuring 84 mm × 268 mm, with vertical chain-lines which are approximately 29 mm apart. On Fol. 80 the banner (made up of two pennants meeting in the centre), has a shaft 56 mm long (including an oval ring of 6–7 mm at its top). The two pennants, each with two waves, of the banner have tips 10 mm apart, and they divide at a point approximately 12 mm up from the banner base and 4 mm in from the shaft. The length of the lower pennant is 27 mm from the shaft to its tip, and that of the upper pennant is 29 mm. These are the same dimensions that are found on the banner watermarks in Harley MS 7650. As the banner and staff in the Harley manuscript are countermarked by 'b–V' with a trefoil, so too, Fol. 79 of Portland MS Pw V 26 appears with a cornermark comprising a trefoil and '–V' motif (from which, unfortunately, the initial element has been cut off along the upper left-hand edge of the paper). The 'V' is approximately 21 mm high and 12 mm wide at its widest point, the same dimensions as its Harley counterpart.[11] It would be unwise to draw too many inferences from such details, but it is possible that the paper Newcastle and his copyists used came from a common source.

The first stock of paper used in Harley MS 7650 is more elusive. The complete figure of the fool's cap, bears some generic resemblance to Heawood's numbers 2061 and 2023, with their long bands tapering down to a trefoil: Heawood's example of the second of these, however, comes from

[10] See especially, the trefoils associated with anchors in Vladimir Mošin, *Anchor Watermarks*, Monumenta Chartæ Papyraceæ Historiam Illustrata 13 (Amsterdam, 1973), nos. 1498–9, 1696, 2105–34.

[11] A similar watermark of a trefoil on a stem with the initial 'V' occurs in Portland MS Pw V 25, Fols. 70–1, containing copies of two songs from *The Variety* in the hand of John Rolleston, see *Dramatic Works by William Cavendish*, ed. Lynn Hulse, Malone Society Reprints (Oxford, 1996), pp. xxi, 148. Another manuscript, BL Add. MS 45865, containing the prose comedy 'Witts Triumvirate or the Philosopher', with the date 1635 on its title-page, was copied by John Rolleston and corrected by the Duke of Newcastle, see Hilton Kelliher, 'Donne, Jonson, Richard Andrews and The Newcastle Manuscript', *English Manuscript Studies* 4 (1993), 134–73 (150, 152). Its watermark consists of a similar banner and staff, but three large letters 'C', 'B', and a reversed '3', perhaps representing 'Z', are attached to the staff.

With these exceptions, no similar watermarks can be found in other Newcastle-related manuscripts, which are all folios: BL, Harl. MS 4955 (The Newcastle Manuscript), BL, Harl. MS 7367 (*The Humorous Lovers*), BL, Add. MS 32497 ('Phanseys'), and Worcester College, Oxford, MSS Plays 9. 21 (*The Court Secret*).

Olfert Dapper's *Afrikaensche Gewesten* (Amsterdam, 1676), dating from considerably later than the manuscript. Yet, unlike Heawood's examples, the cap itself has five points and hence belongs, as Heawood demonstrated elsewhere, to the commonest category of types found in English and Dutch papers during the second half of the century.[12] The other elements in the watermark, 'E D' and what may be the letter 'L', help little to identify the age or origins of the paper. The watermark of the additional leaf (Fol. 78+) consists of a circle which has been filled; unfortunately, the image is so indistinct and the ink so densely written over it, that it is impossible to see of what it consists.

Hands, Scribes, and Substantive Changes

An initial inspection of Harley MS 7650 suggests it contains the work of four distinct hands. The first (Hand 1), in which the bulk of the text is written, offers a clear, semi-calligraphic style which is predominantly italic, but admits secretary and Greek *e*, long *s*, and other occasional features in free variation. Characteristically, the script is inclined slightly to the right and there are a number of distinctive letter-forms: including *r* with a small right-hand basal spur; *p*, *k* and capital *l* with curved feet which extend below the line; *d* with ascenders looping over to the left; and *i* dotted to the right (or, occasionally, to the left) of the stem. The scribe particularly favoured an otiose stroke, slightly resembling a *c* above and to the right of double *ff*s, as in 'staff' (line 460), 'affaires' (line 466), 'huffiñg' (line 1017), and so on; but it occasionally occurs after a single *f* as in 'footeman' (line 575) and 'satisfied' (line 2297), and after the *t* in 'Fift' (line 2117).

Hand 1 is comparatively free of scribal errors: its self-corrections and deletions (which are often made in neat, single strokes) betray evidence of the kinds of mistake of simple repetition or omission that tend to occur even in careful, high-quality, transcriptions. The scribe has the distinctive habit of beginning a speech by copying only a few words on its first line before filling the space available in subsequent lines. Sometimes he may copy only one word (for example, at 257); on one occasion, beginning a speech at 1807, he wrote four words, then seems to have deleted the last two, and copied them again at the beginning of the next line, as if it were essential they did not appear on the first line. These short lines may have been intended to have a dramatic effect—about half of them are not followed by a mark of punctuation—but it is unclear why they occur with such frequency.[13] Two speeches

[12] Edward Heawood, 'Papers Used in England after 1600. I. The Seventeenth Century to c.1680', 4, *The Library*, 11 (1930), 262–99 (278–9); and, see also H. Voorn, *De papiermolens in de provincie Gelderland*, De geschiedenis der Nederlandse papierindustrie 3 (Harlem, 1985), pp. 169, 176.

[13] Short initial lines, of which some are, of course, a matter of interpretation, occur at (an asterisk indicates that the line ends with a mark of punctuation): 178*, 257*, 261*, 265*, 334*, 344, 378*, 388, 405, 429, 505*, 533*, 556, 577, 671*, 812*, 876*, 906, 917*, 928, 942*, 953*, 1002, 1010, 1142*, 1161, 1456, 1462*, 1477*, 1484, 1625*, 1729, 1731, 1751*, 1762*, 1784, 1791, 1807, 1847, 1857*, 1867*, 1874, 1879*, 1883, 1900*, 1910*, 2046*, 2137*, 2154, 2156, 2164*, 2232, 2296, 2321*, 2327*, 2345*, 2404, 2554, 2558, 2715*. The apparent short line at 1297 may be explained by the absence of a speech-prefix for line 1298, supplied by the printed edition of 1649.

have short lines (209, 692) within them: the first ends with a point and virgule, the second with a point and a dash. Although the scribe copied the play continuously, not leaving blank lines around stage-directions or beginning new acts on new pages, he was fairly lavish with paper, writing, for example, each of the orders in 1279–87 on a new line.

Ignoring pages which begin an act, where headings are written in a larger script, most pages contain between sixteen and eighteen lines of text (that is, not including catchwords). The scribe seems to have thought seventeen lines were the correct number for the page, though he occasionally went up to twenty (Fols. 3a–b, 20b, 23b, and 76b)—these 'long' pages, apart from Fols. 3b and 76b, end with a virgule—and on three pages (Fols. 34a, 35a–b) managed no more than fifteen lines. The rectos of Fols. 2a–16a have been ruled for speech-prefixes: the rules are approximately 7 mm apart and do not extend fully to the top of the page. Catchwords appear irregularly throughout the manuscript on both rectos and versos. Entry stage-directions are regularly centered and exits ranged right; some stage-directions, such as 'within' (lines 1657, 1676, 1690) and 'looking forth' (line 1083) have been written in the left-hand margin. There are sets of line-fillers at lines 703, 705, and 1531.

A more spiky secretary hand, using a generally darker ink, wrote over, or supplied interlinings above Hand 1's alterations (see Plates 1–2). This hand (Hand 2), used small, printed characters and was responsible for the majority of the substantive changes made to the text. Its deletions tend to take the form of neat hatchings, sometimes over the single-line cancellations of Hand 1. A close examination of the use of darker ink and its association with these changes suggests that Hand 2 is in all probability responsible for the meticulous revision of punctuation which may be observed throughout the main body of the manuscript.[14] Among its changes appear to be the addition of two ampersands at lines 205 and 652: these take a conventional, modern form, whereas the ampersands of Hand 1 consist of secretary forms, that is of a loop attached to a secretary *z*, resembling the number 3 (see lines 208, 531, 591, and 710). The scribe of Hand 2 also seems to have favoured the use of a ligature when he inserted *st* into the text: the letters are joined in 'wouldst' (line 84), 'constant' (line 900) ''gainst' (line 1196), 'Costiue' (line 1306), and perhaps in 'strangest' (line 1671). Hand 1 formed looping tyldes, rather like horizontal question-marks, with the upper right-hand tail often inked over. There are, however, a certain number of tyldes which take the form of a more-or-less straight line, as in 'ĩnocence' (line 691), 'Com̄on wealth' (line 777), 'com̄and' (line 803), 'stratagem̄e' (line 1463), and

[14] Compare, for example, the ink coloration for the alterations on Fol. 7b (lines 236–9, 243, and 251). Quills tend to leave darker, more concentrated, ink deposits in the short stabbing strokes associated with the formation of stops and commas (Fol. 67b offers a good example of these effects in the ink that is being used by Hand 1). However, it is clear from the case of Fol. 22a that the markedly deeper intensity of Hand 2's ink is often responsible for changes in surrounding punctuation, such as the 'double dotting' of *i* by placing a point above the minim where the original Hand 1 point is too far to the right or left, or is indistinct (see 'in', line 738). Hand 2 could accordingly be interpreted as the interpolating hand supplying the darker ink on pages in which these or other features—such as commas, stops, short virgules—are double marked.

'Nin̄iūie' (line 2533). On four occasions, with 'im̄ediatlie' (line 310), 'win̄e' (line 754), and 'Pin̄s' (twice in line 1679), these straight-line tyldes have two short strokes, resembling double apostrophes, through them. These differently formed tyldes may represent the work of Hand 2: Lavis interpreted the stroked-through tyldes as having been deleted, but they are printed in full in this edition.

A third hand (Hand 3) occurs more rarely, though no less clearly (see Plate 3). Relative to the rest of the text, its character is distinctive: large and sprawling, its predominantly secretary letter-forms are rather untidy. Unlike the neat lineation of Hand 1 or the alterations of Hand 2, Hand 3's corrections are often angled upwards from left to right: deletions are in bold single strokes.

The bulk of the additional leaf (Fol. 78+) is in a fourth hand (Hand 4), different again from that of the main body of the manuscript, and which—possibly on account of the more substantial size of the sheet—has a larger, looser, and more elaborate appearance than either Hand 1 or Hand 2 (see Plate 4). The additional leaf is written using a dark ink, with hatched deletions, and in a professional largely italic style with secretary *e*. It employs the otiose stroke, slightly resembling a *c* above and to the right of the double *s* in 'grosser' (line 1546) and *f* in 'from' (line 1551), and 'fiction' (line 1557), and ligatured *st* in 'thickest' (line 1548), 'Gestures' (line 1551), 'lusty' (line 1552), and 'Masters' (line 1562).

Taking only the clearest examples, and ignoring punctuation and brackets for the moment, the distribution of hands throughout the manuscript can be summarized as follows:

Hand	Folio
H1	1a–78b
H2	7b–8a; 13a–b; 20b–21a; 22a–b; 31a
H3	24b; 38a; 50b; 60a; 62b; 68b; 78+b
H4	78+a–b

The significance of this distribution can be brought out by looking at the identities of the scribes. W. W. Greg pointed out long ago that Hand 3 is Newcastle's autograph. Hilton Kelliher has shown that Hand 4 represents the script of John Rolleston, Newcastle's secretary from the late 1630s to the early 1640s. Peter Beal has recently confirmed Greg's observation that Hand 1 is the hand of the unknown scribe who in the same period copied out the only extant manuscript of James Shirley's play, *The Court Secret*.[15] The evidence suggests, then, a manuscript prepared by Hand 1, corrected by Hand 2, with a scene restored by Rolleston and some revisions by Newcastle: it is a fair copy which may have been originally intended for publication and which—with the exception of a number of changes—must have borne a close relation to the copy-text used in the preparation of the 1649 edition.

[15] Greg, *Dramatic Documents from the Elizabethan Playhouses*, i. 347, 363; Kelliher, 'Donne, Jonson, Richard Andrews and The Newcastle Manuscript', p. 150; Peter Beal, *Index of English Literary Manuscripts: Volume II: 1625–1700*, 2 parts (London, 1987–93), part ii. 324–5, ShJ 175.

Since it is responsible for many of the substantive changes in the manuscript, Hand 2 warrants a little more consideration. Its letter-forms are often very close to those of Hand 1: because they usually appear as interlinear additions, they are smaller and more secretary-hand-like in character, particularly with a frequently marked Greek *e* in contrast to Hand 1's tendency to use a two-stroke form. A certain scribal mobility in the formation of letters—particularly when moving from a cursive hand to the constraints of a smaller, printed style—was not uncommon in the middle of the seventeenth century: the most probable interpretation of Hand 2 is, accordingly, that it represents a more formal version of Hand 1, added in darker ink at a later date, under authorial supervision. The absence of Hand 2 from the manuscript of *The Court Secret* may show Newcastle regarded it differently from the manuscript of *The Country Captain*. Indeed, it has been shown that the substantive alterations to *The Court Secret*—several of which prove to be in Shirley's autograph—were made significantly later than when the manuscript was first copied.[16]

[16] The main scribe's role may therefore be seen as having some bearing on the debate about the authorship of *The Country Captain* (although, by its nature, the evidence cannot be conclusive).

R. G. Howarth has shown that *The Court Secret* can be identified in three versions. The first, sometimes known as *Don Manuell*, is the Worcester College, Oxford, copy (MSS Plays 9. 21), whose main scribe was chiefly responsible for *The Country Captain*: both plays probably date from before November 1642, 'when Newcastle took the field'. The second is the printed version of *The Court Secret*, the last of the *Six New Playes* published in 1653: it was entered in the Stationers' Register to Humphrey Moseley on 10 September. The third version, Howarth contends, is that performed by the King's Men in 1664. Deprived of performing rights to his own work because of a dispute with Moseley, the sole copyright holder, Shirley revised *The Court Secret* as *Don Manuell*, creating a 'new play' by making revisions and additions to the Worcester College Manuscript in his own hand; see R. G. Howarth, 'A Manuscript of James Shirley's *Court Secret*', *Review of English Studies*, 7 (1931), 302–13; and '"A Manuscript of James Shirley's *Court Secret*"', *Review of English Studies*, 8 (1932), 203. As Howarth implies, the gap in time in the play's textual history between the scribe's fair copy and Shirley's late remodelling has remained problematic; but it might be illuminated by reference to Newcastle's movements over the same period. For, if both manuscripts of *The Court Secret* and *The Country Captain* had been in Newcastle's rather than Shirley's possession in 1642, then they may well have accompanied the Earl into exile on the Continent, and would not have been available in England until Newcastle's return in May 1660. In his capacity as main copyist of both manuscripts, the scribe may have been in Newcastle's rather than in Shirley's employ, for among the Portland Papers (University of Nottingham, Portland MS Pw V 375) is a copy of Shirley's satire 'The Common-wealth of Birds' which may be in the scribe's hand, see Beal, *Index of English Literary Manuscripts: Volume II: 1625–1700*, part ii. 325, ShJ 12. Shirley, on the other hand, as Anthony Wood reported, was bound by poverty to subsidize his dramatic activities by acting as a 'drudge' or copyist himself, which makes it unlikely that he would have financed the scribe's activities; see Anthony à Wood, *Athenæ Oxonienses*, new edn., ed. Philip Bliss, 4 vols. (London, 1813–20), iii. col. 739. This interpretation would tally with Howarth's observations that 'There is no evidence that Shirley made or allowed transcripts of his manuscript plays', and that although it was not holograph, the Worcester Manuscript 'was almost certainly the only copy existing until the time of revision for publication' (Howarth (1931), p. 302). Such a scenario is, of course, speculative but it nevertheless seems a plausible explanation for Shirley's delay in returning to the Worcester College Manuscript and supplies an important alternative perspective to that proffered by those who would too readily interpret the main scribe's association with *The Court Secret* as evidence for Shirley's authorship of *The Country Captain*.

Autograph corrections (or even holographs of entire texts) do not necessarily denote authorship of passages they amend or transcribe, but they remain the closest textual signs of authorial interaction with a work. Newcastle's emendations to the text of Harley MS 7650 are light, occasional, and evident in the manuscript from Fol. 24b to Fol. 78+b, giving the impression of fine-tuning after the major task of composition had been completed. At this stage in the proceedings, the Earl seems to have focused mainly on the scenes in which Courtwell Junior is conversing with Lady Huntlove's sister (lines 824, 827–9, 1773, 1776, 2188), and it is highly likely that a number of other small changes in their conversation (lines 1867, 2190), as well as a moment when she is addressing Device (line 1220), may also be laid at his doorstep. Elsewhere, Newcastle appears to have added a stage-direction in one of Sir Francis Courtwell's monologues, at the same time as he smoothed and altered an appositive 'extempted' into the formulation 'and tempted' (lines 2088, 2097). He also restored a missing word to one of Dorothy's speeches (line 2388), and made a couple of improvements to Rolleston's transcript of the song inserted in the last gathering of the manuscript (lines 1552–3). A number of these alterations fall within what are—both dramatically and textually—the most effective scenes in the play.

If Newcastle's annotations represent what were, chronologically speaking, the final moments in the creation of Harley MS 7650, it is equally clear that the penultimate stage in the process was Rolleston's transcription of the appended passage on Fol. 78+. Here, a scribal note in the bottom margin of the verso side—'And then begin as was intended,' (line 1565a)—plainly indicates that the leaf was included in order to rectify an omission in the main body of manuscript, which had therefore probably already been copied. Yet this does not necessarily mean that Rolleston was transcribing what Newcastle had already written, for the leaf itself bears signs of consistent revision under authorial guidance. The scene at the beginning of Act IV where the passage was to be inserted was itself substantially altered between the manuscript and the edition of 1649. In Moseley's printed version a gaming song by Shirley was interpolated where the manuscript called, less specifically, for 'A Song i'th tauerne' (line 1488).[17] Nevertheless, all the changes to the Rolleston sheet, which are for the most part concerned with the substitution of a child singer's order for the musicians to play where formerly the manuscript had directed that he himself should sing, survive into the print, with the single exception of what may have been an even later alteration by Newcastle of 'make' into 'putt' (line 1552).

As there is no sign in the main scribe's work that a passage has been omitted from the first scene of Act IV and since there are no indications as to where Rolleston's text may be inserted, the main scribe's contribution to the work was probably finished before the manuscript arrived at its final form. The implication of this is twofold. Hilton Kelliher has established that Rolleston probably did not accompany Newcastle to the Continent in July 1644; it is therefore likely that by then the main scribe had completed his work on the manuscript and Rolleston had added his leaf to it. Indeed, in the light of the fact that from the beginning of 1642 Newcastle would have been

[17] Shirley's poem, 'A Catch', was printed in his *Poems* (London, 1646), p. 51.

preoccupied by the imminent war and would probably have had little time to devote to correcting plays, it is probable that at least the main scribe's contribution was complete by then.[18] In the second place, the bracketing of passages throughout the manuscript (including the addition), presumably for purposes of cutting, must have been done after both the main scribe's contribution and Rolleston's leaf (which it effectively negates) had been finished. This suggests that the manuscript's function may have changed—possibly after 1642, but in all probability after 1644—from that of a presentation or fair copy to that of a working script marked up for an abridged version of *The Country Captain*.

Bracketing

In this edition of the manuscript the physical extent of the brackets has been recorded as accurately as possible. However, the markings themselves do not appear to have been made with absolute precision. Sometimes they seem to indicate merely the approximate limits of a cancelled passage (in which case the brackets are sometimes closed on one side only). On occasions, where large sections of a page have been placed within brackets they extend beyond the likely limits of the excision (as in the case of Fol. 38a, where a bar across the bracket after line 1291 is probably intended to mark the end of the cut). It is also clear that lines of spoken text have been designated for cutting, while—in order to preserve the logic of the altered scenes—a number of entrances and exits within the deleted passages may be presumed to remain. In short, the bracketing seems to have been executed rapidly with an eye to the pragmatics of performance rather than offering a revised version of the text prepared with print in mind. It seems likely that in practice the markings represent the following cuts (line numberings are inclusive):

Act I	lines 4–24, 39–103, 148–50, 207–8, 212–19, 231–45, 313–31, 362–4, 440–1.
Act II	lines 733–42, 786–852, 872–5.
Act III	lines 1161–1238, 1278–91, 1344–1436, 1438.
Act IV	lines 1506–1656, 1723–1881.
Act V	lines 2137–2202.

This would mean that Act I has been pared down from 477 to 339 lines, Act II from 501 to 418 lines, Act III from 508 to 322 lines, Act IV from 630 to 320 lines, and Act V from 625 to 559 lines; in all (disregarding the stage-directions within the excisions), some 790 lines have been removed from the total length of the play and its playing-time reduced by almost one third.

In terms of content the cuts seem, in general, to bear witness to a thoughtful and workable reshaping of the play. They are almost exclusively concerned with trimming the subplot elements relating to the central drama of Sir Francis Courtwell's infatuation with Lady Huntlove: namely, the scenes

[18] Kelliher, 'Donne, Jonson, Richard Andrews and The Newcastle Manuscript', p. 153; Geoffrey Trease, *Portrait of a Cavalier: William Cavendish, First Duke of Newcastle* (London, 1979), pp. 90–4.

involving Captain Underwit and his cronies, and the wooing scenes between Lady Huntlove's sister and her paramours, Courtwell Junior and Device. With respect to Underwit, the reformed Act I accordingly begins *in medias res* with a much curtailed dialogue between the newly appointed Captain and his servant: this preserves the narrative bones of the original scene and allows Underwit a shortened dialogue with Device. Act III minimizes his exchange with Captain Sackbury, diminishing his badinage with the Captain, Engine, and Courtwell Junior; and Act IV discards the larger part of the problematic and static tavern scene (including the Rolleston addition), in which Underwit carouses with his friends.[19] These changes have the effect of reducing Underwit's role in the play until his entry in Act V, but thereafter his uncut romantic entrapment by Mistress Dorothy correspondingly gains a clearer focus.

By contrast, in the case of Lady Huntlove's sister the romantic component is honed down. What is perhaps the central scene of the second act—in which the tongue-tied Courtwell Junior is induced to commence his wooing—is cut from nearly one hundred lines (lines 786–884, inclusive) to twenty-nine (lines 853–72, probably ending on 'the Earth', and 876–84), a change which almost entirely eliminates Courtwell's Neoplatonic register but preserves his legalistic rhetoric intact. Similarly, the fourth act completely dispenses with Courtwell and his lover's drunken psychomachia (lines 1723–1881), as well as cutting the courtly formalism of the transitional scene in Act V which precedes their final reconciliation (lines 2137–2202). The result is that Courtwell is flattened out into a dull, proud, legalistic creature who marries the Sister merely because of her part in the discomfiting of Device. His beloved's personality becomes far more wilful and less intellectual than it is in the original version in which she triumphs with sharpness and grace in her verbal sparring matches.

If the complex characterization of these two figures is simplified in the version of the play produced by the bracketing, so too is the portrait of Device. Throughout, his role is much reduced, not only in his scenes with Underwit, but also in those with Lady Huntlove's sister. In the original version of the play he is characterized by his commentaries on his own fantastical clothing, as well as by his aspirations as a versifier; although the bracketing crops the commentaries, references to and examples of his skills as a songwriter and poet are cut more severely. After his intended has

[19] In this reading, the spoken text begins at line 25 and cuts after Underwit's announcement that he has been made a Captain (line 38) to his acknowledgement that in this role he might require the help of a friend (line 104). The transition is a little abrupt, but it is certainly actable. The dialogue is neatly spliced after Device has offered to march under the ensign of the Captain's favour (lines 205–6), has taken up with Underwit's observation on Device's mode of dress (lines 210–11), and has parried, after the subsequent cut, Device's comments on the fashions controlling his choice of clothing (line 220), which, in turn, are rounded off by a further question about Underwit's captaincy (lines 221–3). The banter scene breaks off immediately after Engine's entry (line 1343), to begin with Sackbury's words on the entry of Sir Francis and Lady Huntlove—'M^{r}. Engin, that gentleman loues you not, come, ile bring vp the rere' (lines 1439–40)—so that Engine's presence here merely serves the function of drawing Underwit and his friends offstage in order that the Lady and her admirer may begin to plan their tryst. The opening scene of Act IV jumps, smoothly enough, from the entry of Underwit and Sackbury (line 1505), to the awakening of Engine from his stupor (line 1658).

invited him to visit the Huntloves in the country (lines 311–12) his response—which advertises his poetic talents—is removed (in an excision which, in all likelihood, runs to as far as the entry of Sir Francis Courtwell in line 332). Once the Sister has concurred with Dorothy (albeit dismissively) that 'yes yes,' Device 'can write verses' (line 732), the two women's following discussion of authors and authorship is removed (lines 733–42). After the entry of the Sister and Device together in Act III, the whole of Device's recitation of his poetry is left out (in a cut which is probably meant to extend from line 1155 to line 1238). Hence the revised scene begins—after a clearly marked close to the bracketing—'Ladie, how do you like the Novice that Sir Richard comended' (lines 1238–9), so that the attention of the audience is focused from the outset on the rivalry between Device and Courtwell Junior. Overall, then, the brackets bear witness to a version of the play in which the more tedious passages have been dropped (most notably Courtwell's railing, Device's recitation, and the bulk of the tavern scene), and in which the complexity of the subplot characters has been drastically reduced. The result is a play which is in some ways more neatly formulated than the original, but in which the moralistic saga of Sir Francis and his thwarted desire for Lady Huntlove gains, by default, a rather overpowering prominence.[20]

In conjunction with the alterations made to the bracketing on lines 1278–91, a hand, writing in the same ink, has smoothed the main scribe's 'So inough' into 'ran tan, enough', adding the first word in the left-hand margin. As this change appears to be in Newcastle's hand, it is probable that he made the cuts marked in the manuscript. A variety of sources show that pieces by Newcastle were performed in Paris and in Antwerp during his exile from England which began in 1644. In fact, as Leslie Hotson has noticed, Newcastle was 'intimately connected' with a company of English actors. The company may have been the one which was at The Hague from (at least) November 1644 to February 1645; it seems to have disbanded by November 1646, and is mentioned in connection with the performance of Newcastle's work in *The Kingdomes Weekly Intelligencer* for 23 February–2 March 1647.[21] The publication of *The Country Captaine* in The Hague in 1649 would, presumably, have obviated the need to mark cuts in the manuscript fair copy. Margaret Lucas, with whom Newcastle was associating after December 1645, does not make any explicit reference to having seen the play. It therefore seems likely that the cut version was created between his arrival in Paris on 20 April 1645 and the end of the year (although there is evidence that his theatrical career in that city extended into 1646).[22] It also seems consistent with such a view, particularly with respect to the possibility that the play was

[20] As such, the cuts would be in keeping with the Duchess of Newcastle's insistence on her husband's moral agenda in his comedies: namely that his chief design was 'to divulge and laugh at the follies of mankind; to persecute vice, and to encourage virtue': see *The Life of William Cavendish, Duke of Newcastle, To Which is Added the True Relation of My Birth Breeding, and Life, By Margaret, Duchess of Newcastle*, ed. C. H. Firth, 2nd edn. (London, [1906]), p. 109.

[21] Leslie Hotson, *The Commonwealth and Restoration Stage* (Cambridge, Mass., 1928), p. 21.

[22] Trease, pp. 145, 153–4.

performed in Paris, that the cuts should have included a jibe about a 'french Lacquey' (line 242), as well as an 'English Monsier' (lines 362–3), in addition to many of the scenes which satirized Device's continental foppery.

Dating

The Country Captain must have been written by 7 August 1641 when it appears in the list of plays of the King's Men which the Earl of Essex, the Lord Chamberlain, sent to the Masters and Wardens of the Stationers' Company to prevent their publication without the company's consent.[23] A reference in the play to 'the league at Barwick, and the late expeditions' (lines 66–7) clearly means it must date from after the signing of the Pacification of Berwick on 18 June 1639: Lavis argued that Device's ballad, 'a pittifull Complaint of the Ladies, when they were banish'd the Towne with their husbands to their Countrey houses' (lines 319–21), related to a proclamation to that effect dated 29 January 1639.[24]

Arguments from common themes can seldom be more than incremental, nevertheless there seems to be a good match between events in the play, other issues in the air in the early 1640s, and what is known of Newcastle's movements. It is clear that the subject-matter of the play is closely bound up with what were from 1639 onwards pressing issues for Newcastle. In that year, as Arthur Collins reported, 'when an Army was to be raised to reduce the Malecontents in *Scotland*, and the Treasury being exhausted, a Supply was desired of the Noblest and Richest of his Loyal Subjects in *England*; his Lordship lent his Majesty 10000 *l*. and raised himself a Volunteer Troop of Horse, of 120 Gentlemen of Quality . . . and marched into Berwick the 30th of *May*'.[25] Further, by detecting echoes of Habington's *The Queen of Aragon* in the 1649 prologue, G. E. Bentley argued that *The Country Captain* may

[23] See *Mercurius Britanicus*, 10–17 February 1645, sig 4B2b; Gerald Eades Bentley, *The Jacobean and Caroline Stage*, 7 vols. (Oxford 1941–68), i. 65–6.

Greg, *A Bibliography of the English Printed Drama to the Restoration*, iii. 1031–2, gives the Stationers' Register entries for *The Country Captain* as follows: 4(?) September 1646, entered to Humphrey Robinson and Humphrey Moseley, 'Country Captaine, Varieties, by my Lord of Newcastle'; 30 January 1673, transferred to John Martin and Henry Herringman, 'Lady Newcastles Country Captaine, halfe, Varieties, halfe'; 21 August 1683, transferred to Robert Scott, 'Lord New Castles Country Capt., Varieties, a fourth'. In the light of Newcastle's association with the English Players in Paris, it is reasonable to suspect that the entry for 4(?) September 1646 and the completion of Harley MS 7650 may have been part of the same enterprise—an interpretation which may find some support in Gerard Langbaine's belief that 'this Play was writ during his Exile', *An Account of the English Dramatick Poets* (Oxford, 1691), p. 386. Certainly, if *The Country Captain* (even in an abridged form) were performed in Paris before the demise of the company, this would help to explain not only the bracketing of the manuscript itself, but also the additional revisions and dramatic improvements which H. T. E. Perry has shown were made between the manuscript and the printed version of 1649—see *The First Duchess of Newcastle and Her Husband as Figures in Literary History* (Boston, Mass., and London, 1918), pp. 103–4. Against Perry's argument, it is likely that in the mid-1640s, and in the absence of Shirley (who did not attend the Earl in his travels on the Continent), actors would have instigated these changes.

[24] Lavis, pp. lxi–lxiii.

[25] Arthur Collins, *Historical Collections of the Noble Families of Cavendishe, Holles, Vere, Harley, and Ogle* (London, 1752), p. 27.

have been produced after April 1640.[26] More specifically, some episodes in the play tally well with the events in June and July 1641 which culminated in a situation whereby—as Quick fretted in *The Stage-Players Complaint* (London, 1641)—'Monopolers are downe, Projectors are downe, the High Comission Court is downe, the Starre-Chamber is down, & (some think) Bishops will downe'.[27] These political events would have given a stinging edge to the satire of Engine's entrepreneurial activities and his insecurities about being hanged for his projective schemes (lines 775, 928–9, 938, 948, 953, 1335, 1374, 1405, 1494, 1673–4, 2517, 2522). In fact, the very monopolies spewed out by Engine at the height of his discomfiture—pins, cards, and dice, soap, hides, wine, and tobacco (lines 1671–1703)—were the same as those which came under renewed attack in the new legislative drives of November 1640: many were still being debated in the following year.[28] References in the play to social unease and the disaffection of the apprentices (lines 1699–1704) would also fit quite naturally into the events of the period, since there was trouble with apprentices on Shrove Tuesday 1641.[29]

Even more suggestively, Captain Underwit's otherwise cryptic jibe that Westminster Hall was a fencing-school in which people 'let one anotherd blood in Lawe' (lines 32–3) fits aptly into the context of Strafford's impeachment which began there on 22 March 1641. The motif of the *causa sanguinis* had been made topical by Oliver St John, late in 1640, in an attempt to dissuade the clergy from intervening on Strafford's behalf. The relocation of the trial in Westminster Hall (on the grounds that the House of Lords was not large enough to accommodate proceedings on such a scale) constituted, in itself, an event unusual enough to attract comment. Strafford had been, of course, a friend of Newcastle's, and the poem the latter wrote on his execution ('Great Strafford, worthy of that name'), bears elegant witness to the

[26] For the dating of the play, see Bentley, *The Jacobean and Caroline Stage*, iii. 147; and for Bentley's discussion of *The Country Captain*, see iii. 145–51.

[27] *The Stage-Players Complaint* (London, 1641), p. 4; for the dating of this tract see Bentley, *The Jacobean and Caroline Stage*, i. 65, n. 2.

[28] For monopolies during this period, see, for example, the *Calendar of State Papers, Domestic Series*, 1640, pp. 97–8; 1640–1, pp. 252–3, 259–61, 263–4, 271, 563–4; and John Rushworth, *Historical Collections*, 4 parts in 8 vols. (London, 1659–1701), part 3, vol. 1 (London 1692), p. 165 (February 1641). A parallel to Engine's involvement in the soap business may be found in the character of Mihil, Crossewill's son, in Richard Brome's *The Weeding of the Covent Garden* (1632), which was revived in 1641 (with a dedicatory encomium on Newcastle himself), and gained an even greater sharpness in its new context. For further discussions of the soap monopoly, see *Calendar of State Papers, Domestic Series*, 1631–3, p. 366; William Hyde Price, *The English Patents of Monopoly* (Boston, Mass., and New York, 1906), pp. 119–28; Margaret James, *Social Problems and Policy During the Puritan Revolution: 1640–1660* (London, 1930), pp. 131–44; and R. J. Kaufmann, *Richard Brome: Caroline Playwright* (New York and London, 1961), pp. 69–70.

[29] See K. J. Lindley, 'Riot Prevention and Control in Early Stuart England', 5, *Transactions of the Royal Historical Society*, 33 (1983), pp. 109–26 (109–10, n. 2). The Shrove Tuesday disruptions of the apprentices were, however, almost proverbial by this time, see *Calendar of State Papers, Domestic Series*, 1640, p. 190.

keenness with which he was following the events of that spring.[30] It is also tempting to speculate on whether there may have been a relationship between the twist in the plot of Sir Francis Courtwell's fall from a horse and his broken shoulder in the final act of the play (lines 2612–41), and the fate of Newcastle's charge, Prince Charles, who sustained a similar injury from a similar tumble in June 1641. The incident released Newcastle from his immediate responsibilities as governor to the Prince while he convalesced with his mother, and came to signal (for quite other reasons) the end of the Earl's offices in that coveted capacity.[31] He was presumably then free for such projects as the completion of a play.

That the early summer season of 1641 would have been the most appropriate time for the initial staging of *The Country Captain* is suggested even more strongly by another internal reference. In Act V, Courtwell Junior informs Lady Huntlove of his wedding to her sister by announcing, 'we haue been at, I Iohn take the Elizabeth' (line 2574). Since there is no indication elsewhere in the play that Courtwell Junior is called John (or the Sister, Elizabeth), and since these names were not commonly associated with the marriage-pledge, it seems likely that the passage constitutes a playful allusion to the wedding of Newcastle's daughter, Elizabeth, to John Egerton, Viscount Brackley, on 22 July 1641. In the light of Egerton's dramatic role as the Elder Brother in *Comus* seven years earlier (as well as his position as its eventual dedicatee), the reference would appear to be reinforced by the promise of a masque at line 2603, and the 'reuells' anticipated by Courtwell Junior at the end of the play (line 2729).[32] An allusion with such a local resonance would have had little effect more than a few weeks either side of the wedding itself. Since plague appears to have necessitated the closing of the London theatres from 5 August until the last week of November, it is reasonable to speculate that the play was performed sooner rather than later, at some point between May and August. The title-page of the first printing specified that the comedy was presented at the Blackfriars Theatre by the King's Men. Their custom was to move from the Blackfriars to the Globe for the summer: if *The Country Captain* had its original production at the Blackfriars, it could not have been performed much later than 19 May, when Sir Humphrey Mildmay attended a play there.[33] On the other hand, it is at least as likely that the comedy could have been broken in at the Globe and consolidated at the Blackfriars in the winter season of the same year.

[30] C. V. Wedgwood, *Thomas Wentworth, First Earl of Strafford 1593–1641: A Revaluation* (London, 1961; rpt. 1971), pp. 232, 332; for Wentworth's friendship with Newcastle, see pp. 90, 167. Newcastle's poem on Strafford may be found among the Portland Papers, copied out in Rolleston's hand (Portland MS Pw V 25, Fol. 29).

[31] See Trease, pp. 86–7.

[32] The correct date for the wedding is given by William Riley Parker, *Milton: A Biography*, 2 vols. (Oxford, 1968), ii. 790–1. See also Willa McClung Evans, *Henry Lawes, Musician and Friend of Poets* (New York, 1941), pp. 166, 172 n. 2, 191.

[33] Bentley, *The Jacobean and Caroline Stage*, ii. 679.

'It is unfortunate,' wrote the envenomed F. G. Fleay of A. H. Bullen in 1891, 'that this gentleman will rush in with rash assertions where sound critics fear to tread. His special delight is to set up ninepin hypotheses, and then bowl them down again. But no doubt it pays him and his publisher.' Fleay's pique was probably precipitated by an attack which, as he reveals some lines later, Bullen had 'anonymously' delivered against him in the pages of the *Athenaeum*. More specifically, the object of his critical scorn was Bullen's edition of *The Country Captain* which had been published eight years previously—in line with Halliwell's renaming of the untitled play in Harley MS 7650—as *Captain Underwit*. Fleay fixed his primary sights on Bullen's statement in the edition that 'it is absolutely certain . . . *Captain Underwit* is a comedy of Shirley's', but he also targeted the editor's culpability for a number of factual failings which found their way into the notes.[34]

In many respects, these charges were justified. Bullen does seem to have erred, as Fleay alleged, in the details he supplied about individuals (such as Parsons, Tarleton, and Webster) relevant to the play. In the introduction to the play Bullen contrasted his own situation with that of an editor 'with plenty of leisure on his hands':[35] the suspicion arises that he may have completed the edition in haste. This is certainly the general impression furnished by its misreadings or mistranscriptions of, for example, 'him' for 'tyme' (line 913), 'write' for 'invite' (line 1268), 'intend' for 'meane' (line 1369), 'Constables' for 'Constable' (line 1416), '*Un.*' for 'Dra:' (line 1720), 'sucklegge' for 'suckegge' (line 2124); by its additions, such as 'helpe me to' for 'helpe to' (line 1695); and by its omissions, which include 'still for' instead of 'still, marry for' (lines 1419–20), 'deliver'd to' for 'deliue'rd so to' (line 1448), 'Nay, take' for 'Nay nay take' (line 1636), 'come up' for 'come all vp' (lines 1674–5), 'the' for 'o'the' (line 1704), 'too't, not' for 'toot, no, not' (line 1735), and by the dropping of the question, 'are wee all of one Religion?' (lines 1430–1).

It also seems clear that an *a priori* assumption of Shirley's authorship skewed Bullen's reading of allusions in the play. In a note in Act I, for example, he compares Sir Richard Huntlove's speech on the joys of the country (lines 143–72) with the opening lines of Shirley's comedy, *The Lady of Pleasure*, but he fails to notice Newcastle's strikingly similar exposition on the same subject in his book of advice to Charles II.[36] In Act II, Bullen pounces on 'leuerets' (line 564), inviting the reader to remember a comparable use of the word in Shirley's later moral allegory, *Honoria and Mammon* (London, 1659), without reflecting on the ubiquity of the term in the period, and without an apparent awareness that its transferred senses were in use from at least 1617 onwards.[37] Later in the same act, where Sir Francis is seeking to

[34] F. G. Fleay, *A Biographical Chronicle of the English Drama 1559–1642*, 2 vols. (London, 1891), i. 48–9.

[35] *Captain Underwit*, p. 315.

[36] *Captain Underwit*, p. 324, n. 1; see Bodleian Library, MS Clarendon 109, Fols. 74–5.

[37] For the Shirleyan connection, see *Captain Underwit*, p. 340, n. 2; or the *OED*, 'leveret' 2. The association of women with leverets seems also to have been familiar throughout Cavalier literature, finding perhaps its most memorable expression in Edmund Waller's 'Of a Tree Cut in Paper', *Poems* (London, 1668), p. 233.

persuade his sweetheart that they should 'make lawes to loue, teach tyme new motion, or chaine him with the cordage of his haire' (lines 913–14), Bullen—with a triumphant '*Aut Shirley aut Diabolus*'—seizes on the passage for comparison with a similar image in Shirley's play, *The Duke's Mistress*:[38] his mistranscription of 'tyme' as 'him' altering the resonance of the lines and perhaps blinding him to a due recognition of the fact that the conceit of taking time by the forelock was no more than a commonplace.

At this level, then, Bullen's case for Shirley's authorship seems to be based on little more than guesswork. One could no more conclude by such an argument that the work is Shirley's than one could infer from *The Varietie*—with its jeerers, magnetic ladies, women's academies, 'engineers' and all the other paraphernalia of later Jonsonian comedy—that *The Country Captain*'s companion piece was by Jonson, long dead, of course, by the time of its first performance. Further, there is a good deal of historical detail, both external and internal to Harley MS 7650, which would support the attribution of the play to Newcastle. In the first place, the attribution would seem to be circumstantially corroborated by the fact that the initial printing of the play in Holland, by the English bookseller and Royalist, Samuel Browne, 'dwelling', at the time, 'in the Achter-Om at the signe of the English Printing Press', coincided with Newcastle's own movements subsequent to his exile from England after his retreat from the battle of Marston Moor. Newcastle based himself in Rotterdam over the summer of 1648, when the volume must have been in preparation, and visited The Hague (where Prince Charles was temporarily holding court) before his departure to Antwerp in October of the same year.[39] Although the title-page of the 1649 publication of *The Country Captaine* with *The Varietie* described them as having been written by 'a Person of *HONOR*', the entry in the Stationers' Register for 4(?) September 1646 recorded them as 'by my Lord of Newcastle'.[40] In some verses prefacing William Cartwright's *Comedies, Tragi-Comedies, with other Poems* Joseph Leigh put forward the claim that, among the plays printed by Humphrey Moseley, 'fam'd NEVVCASTLE'S choice *Variety*, | With his brave *Captain* held up *Poetry*'.[41] In two contemporary catalogues, by Edward Archer in 1656 and by Francis Kirkman in 1661, the play is assigned to the Earl of Newcastle.[42] Finally, Restoration testimony is on Newcastle's side. On 26 October 1661, Samuel Pepys—who was to see *The Country Captain* on at least four occasions over the next seven years (each time without enthusiasm)—commented that it was 'a play of my Lord Newcastles'.[43] From a

[38] *Captain Underwit*, p. 353, n. 1. Other parallels between *The Country Captain* and Newcastle's and Shirley's writings are noted by Lavis, pp. lxiv–ciii.

[39] For Samuel Browne, see Henry R. Plomer, *A Dictionary of the Booksellers and Printers who were at work in England, Scotland and Ireland from 1641 to 1667* (London, 1907), p. 36. For Newcastle's movements at this time, see Collins, *Historical Collections*, p. 37 and Trease, pp. 159–60.

[40] See above n. 23.

[41] William Cartwright, *Comedies, Tragi-Comedies, with other Poems* (London, 1651), fol. [vii].

[42] Greg, *A Bibliography of the English Printed Drama to the Restoration*, iii. 1331, 1342.

[43] *The Diary of Samuel Pepys*, ed. Robert Latham and William Matthews, 11 vols. (London, 1970–83), ii. 202 (26 October 1661); ii. 220 (25 November, 1661); viii. 385–6 (14 August 1667); ix. 198–9 (14 May 1668).

slightly later period, among the surviving manuscripts from Newcastle's library at Welbeck Abbey (now part of the Portland Papers), there is a 'Prologue Or Epilogue To The Country Captain', written in praise of its 'Noble Authour' by Thomas Shadwell for a revival of the play belonging, in all probability, to the early 1680s.[44] With the onset of the next decade, Gerard Langbaine the Younger, amid a five-page encomium on the late Duke and his work, reiterated the praises of Leigh (supplemented by those of Brome and Shadwell) and credited Newcastle with having written 'four Comedies, which have always been acted with applause; *viz. Country Captain . . . Humorous Lovers, . . . Triumphant Widow*, [and] *Variety*'.[45]

It is equally clear that before 1646 Newcastle had already gained something of a reputation—among friends and detractors alike—as a playwright. In February 1645 the Parliamentary news-sheet *Mercurius Britanicus* mocked the Earl as 'one that in time of peace tired the stage in *Black-Fryers* with his *Comedies*: and afterwards, one that trode the stage in the *North* with the first *Tragedies*'. This note was taken up by several other pamphleteers and seems to allude to *The Varietie* and *The Country Captain*, since both of them—as the title-page of the 1649 edition suggests—were performed at the Blackfriars.

The weight of the internal and external evidence argues in favour of Newcastle's authorship, while the bulk of Bullen's case for Shirley's composition of *The Country Captain* is very frail. These considerations, however, do not preclude the possibility that Shirley, in his capacity as chief dramatist for the King's Men between 1640 and 1642, may have corrected and adapted Newcastle's manuscript for the stage: this is, in essence, Lavis's view of the nature of the collaboration for which she argues.[46] After all, playwrights such as Dryden and Shadwell certainly did aid Newcastle in the completion of his later plays. In view of Anthony Wood's claim, that 'Our author Shirley did also much assist his generous patron William duke of Newcastle in the composure of certain plays, which the duke afterwards published', it seems reasonable to suspect that the final text of *The Country Captain* was created with the help of a professional dramatist.[47] Further, thanks to a discovery by Nigel Bawcutt, we now know that in 1641 Shirley was paid for 'several reformations' made to *The Varietie*: it would accordingly seem highly probable that Shirley had contributed in like manner to its companion piece.[48]

Yet reformation of a text is a very different matter from authorship.

[44] University of Nottingham, Portland MS Pw V 370, see Beal, *Index of English Literary Manuscripts: Volume II: 1625–1700*, part ii, SdT 14. The dating of Shadwell's autograph poem is implicit in its opening lines: 'A Good Play cannot properly be sed/To be reviv'd, because it ne're was dead:/Though it seem buried, like the fruitfull Grain,/It allways rises with Increase againe./So Rises this; whose Noble Authour drew/Such Images, so pleasing and so true,/That after forty yeares they still are new'.

[45] *An Account of the English Dramatick Poets*, p. 386.

[46] Lavis, pp. cii–ciii.

[47] Wood, iii. col. 739.

[48] *The Control and Censorship of Caroline Drama: The Records of Sir Henry Herbert, Master of the Revels 1623–73*, ed. N. W. Bawcutt (Oxford, 1996), p. 209; Herbert records in the same note 'My Lo^{d} Newcastle, as it is said hath some hand in it.' This finding modifies Perry's sneer (p. 113) that *The Varietie* 'is always published with *The Country Captain*, but one would not insult Shirley by suggesting that he is responsible for any part in it'.

Besides the plural marker ('plays') in Wood's comment and the ambiguous status of the main scribe who also copied *The Court Secret*, the only direct link associating Harley MS 7650 with Shirley is the single epigrammatic line (dropped in the 1649 version) concerning the horse 'that snorts at Spaine, by an instinct of Nature' (line 2534). This is from Shirley's earlier comedy of 1633, *The Bird in a Cage* (sig. G4a); but since, as Arthur Collins recorded, Newcastle was an 'excellent Master of the Art of *Manage*' (he was praised by the usually contemptuous Horace Walpole for publishing 'a magnificent Work on that Subject'),[49] the line is at least as likely to have been savoured and cited by Newcastle as it is to have been rehashed by Shirley from an old play. As it stands, such an allusion is no more an index of authorship than are the analogues and echoes from Dekker, Fletcher, Goffe, Jonson, Shakespeare, and Webster (as well as Shirley), which were noticed by Forsythe in the early years of the present century.[50] The problem of attribution, then, lies not so much in proving the probable fact of Shirley's involvement with the play as with determining, on the available evidence, the extent of his contribution.

At the extreme end of the scale in the debate over this question is Bullen. Four years after the publication of his edition, he acknowledged in 1887 that he was wrong to believe that in Harley MS 7650 he had rediscovered a lost play by Shirley. He retracted his belief that Shirley was the sole author of what he had previously called a 'lively comedy', citing Pepys's judgement instead that it was a 'silly' play, as well as Wood's statement of Shirley's involvement in its composition. Bullen substituted an amended claim (without putting forward any new evidence) that *The Country Captain* was 'mainly written by Shirley'.[51] This view has been accepted by a number of subsequent commentators, most markedly by H. T. E. Perry in 1918, and has been invoked more recently in Lynn Hulse's note that Shirley was reputed to have taken 'the lion's share' in the composition of *The Country Captain*).[52] On the other hand, Alexander Dyce, who was well attuned to Shirley's style, had been sceptical about the mere presence of Shirley's hand

[49] See Collins, *Historical Collections*, p. 40; the British Library copy (1322. ff. 8.) has Walpole's marginalia.

[50] R. S. Forsythe, *The Relations of Shirley's Plays to the Elizabethan Drama* (1915; rpt. New York, 1965), pp. 426–9.

[51] A. H. Bullen, *The Works of Thomas Nabbes*, 2 vols. (London, 1887), i. ix–x.

[52] Lynn Hulse, 'Apollo's Whirligig: William Cavendish, Duke of Newcastle and his Music Collection', *The Seventeenth Century,* 9 (1994), 230; and Perry, pp. 102–12. Perry unfairly constructed a scenario whereby Newcastle 'who had recently developed a penchant for dramatic writing' surreptitiously paid Shirley off for effectively surrendering his now lost play, *Look to the Lady,* to pass off as his own with the addition merely of a few 'low comic scenes where any poetic feeling would have been superfluous'. In view of the fact that *Look to the Lady* could be invoked as the possible title of virtually any romantic comedy of the seventeenth century from *Twelfth Night* to *The Constant Couple*, it is probably as well to accept Perry's own verdict that such an interpretation of the evidence 'is romancing, and whatever truth may be in it, there is no proof thereof' (p. 112).

in either of the plays.[53] In terms of style it is, indeed, difficult to arrive at criteria which could be used as a means clearly to assign specific sections of the play to Shirley, rather than to Newcastle. Distinctive negatives such as 'wonot' and 'shan(n)ot' are a case in point. Although they both occur throughout Harley MS 7650 and may occasionally be found in Shirley's dramas,[54] their general absence from the 1649 printing of *The Country Captaine* underlines the likelihood that they probably reflect the preferred forms of the main scribe who had, of course, also transcribed some of Shirley's work, or of some other intermediary, rather than those of any particular author. The same argument could be applied, naturally enough, to other forms, such as 'buoy' (line 571), which Bullen and Forsythe attributed to Shirley and Shakespeare, respectively.[55] Nor, in this context, do lexical items offer the possibility of a diagnostic clarity much above the scribal level. The related terms 'mode' and 'alamode', for example, which would seem to feature in Harley MS 7650 as the earliest recorded uses of these senses in English, certainly had a special meaning elsewhere for Newcastle.[56] On the other hand, the presence of the character, Alamode, in Shirley's *Honoria and Mammon*—albeit a decade after the publication of *The Country Captaine*—obstructs any easy identification of the word with the unique output of either dramatist.[57] Textual problems associated with collaboration are present in all Newcastle's printed plays: the absence, at the present time, of a database containing sufficient material unequivocally by the Earl makes the comparison of like materials with like not yet viable as a reliable means of determining authorship through stylistic resemblance.

[53] Dyce, discussing Wood's comment, wrote: 'The style of his Grace's dramas would certainly have induced me to suspect the truth of this statement, if I had not discovered, that a drinking-song, which is inserted in the Duke's comedy, called *The Country Captain*, is printed among our author's POEMS', *The Dramatic Works and Poems of James Shirley*, ed. William Gifford and Alexander Dyce, 6 vols. (London, 1833; reissued New York, 1966) i. xliii. The song, first printed 1646, does not occur in Harley MS 7650; it therefore supplies no more than marginal evidence to claims for Shirley's authorship of *The Country Captain*. Rather, it would seem sensible to assume that on seeing the direction 'A Song' in the play, Shirley—who was in 1641 the King's Men's leading dramatist (see Bentley, *The Jacobean and Caroline Stage*, i. 63)—substituted one of his own. Lynn Hulse, 'Apollo's Whirligig: William Cavendish, Duke of Newcastle, and his Music Collection', pp. 230, 244, has shown that the song was set by Henry Lawes and seems to have enjoyed some popularity over the period. It would have been natural, especially in the light of the composer's association elsewhere with the Cavendish family (see n. 32)—to include it in the 1649 edition.

[54] For 'wonot', see lines 461, 467, 494, 498, and so on; for 'shanot', see lines 432, 2036, 2523; for 'shannot', see line 1795; see also 'shat' lines 105, 2624. Cf., for instance, 'wonot ruine' in *The Lady of Pleasure* (London, 1637), sig. I4b. The subject is discussed by Lavis, pp. xcviii–c.

[55] *Captain Underwit*, p. 338, n. 1; Forsythe, p. 426.

[56] *OED*, 'mode' *sb*. 9 and 'à la mode' 1. See Martin Butler, *Theatre and Crisis, 1632–1642* (Cambridge, 1984), p. 195; and *A Catalogue of Letters and other Historical Documents Exhibited in the Library at Welbeck* (London, 1903), compiled by Sandford Arthur Strong, p. 213.

[57] Similarly, Forsythe, p. 427, also commented significantly on the word 'rotten' (Harley MS 7650, line 1294; conjectured as 'rooted' by Bullen in *Captain Underwit*, p. 366), mentioning that it occurs in *The Humorous Courtier* (III. i) and *The Constant Maid* (III. ii), with the meaning 'to have by heart'. In fact the *OED* does not recognize Forsythe's conjecture here and classifies the Shirleyan references merely as meaning 'More than ripe' (*OED*, 'rotten' *a*. 9), so that the point—ingenious though it is—begins to lose itself in the instabilities of figurative interpretation.

Scholars have identified several idiosyncratic scribal practices in Newcastle's autograph works. Reproducing the manuscript of 'A Songe' ('Prethee butt heare-mee'), P. J. Croft pointed out that Newcastle 'uses only commas but is fairly liberal with those'. In the manuscript of *The Country Captain* the scribe consistently uses a comma or short virgule where a full-stop or longer virgule might be expected. Croft also commented on Newcastle's unusual use of the tylde over terminal *n*: 'Sun̄' (1949) appears in the manuscript, as do 'Drum̄s' (85) and 'Gun̄s' (87).[58] Lynne Hulse has identified Newcastle's fondness—not unusual in the period—for 'the unetymological word division involving the separation of the first letter of words beginning with *a* from the rest of the word'.[59] The following examples of this practice can be found in *The Country Captain*: 'a bout' (218, 486), 'a broad' (1852), 'a like' (1019), 'a sleepe' (1086, 1093, 2038, 2050, 2054), and 'a way' or 'A way' (1026, 1135, 1328, 1393, 2677, 2702).

Recent studies of Newcastle and his circle have begun to see him as a more creative and productive individual than had been suggested by commentators earlier in the twentieth century. The evidence of *Love's Triumvirate* demonstrates that by the early 1640s he was not entirely new to dramatic composition. Even if the Duchess of Newcastle's judgement that he was 'the best lyric and dramatic poet of this age' seems wrong, the sheer quantity of poetic and dramatic work in his own and Rolleston's hands among the Portland Papers testifies eloquently enough to the seriousness of his literary endeavour.[60] Lynn Hulse, reappraising the respective contributions of Newcastle and Shadwell to the collaborative comedy *The Triumphant Widow* in view of its reappropriation of passages from Newcastle's earlier work, 'The King's Entertainment' of about 1660, has concluded of the play that 'the Duke had a greater part in its authorship than literary historians have previously allowed'.[61] In the face of Newcastle's clear autograph corrections to Harley MS 7650 and in the absence of any clear evidence in favour of conflicting authorial claims, the same verdict could now stand for *The Country Captain*.

Editorial Conventions

In this semi-diplomatic edition the following conventions have been observed. Square brackets enclose deletions, except those around folio numbers ([Fol. 1a] etc.). Angle brackets enclose material which other causes (paper damage, blotting) have removed or made difficult or impossible to decipher. In such cases, dots indicate illegible characters (thus ⟨.⟩). Each line of text—including cancelled lines, act divisions, speech-prefixes, and stage-

[58] P. J. Croft, *Autograph Poetry in the English Language*, 2 vols. (London, 1973), i. no. 35.

[59] *Dramatic Works by William Cavendish*, pp. xx–xxi.

[60] *The Life of William Cavendish, Duke of Newcastle, By Margaret, Duchess of Newcastle*, pp. 108–9. For a summary of recent evaluations of Newcastle's achievements, see Timothy Raylor's Preface to *The Seventeenth Century*, Special Issue: *The Cavendish Circle* 9, no. 2 (Autumn 1994), 141–4.

[61] Lynn Hulse, '"The King's Entertainment" by the Duke of Newcastle', *Viator*, 26 (1995), 355–405: the quotation is from the summary of the article on p. x.

directions—is numbered separately; the text as a whole is numbered continuously. Catchwords and interlineations of one or two words are excluded from the line-count. Scribal comment, catchwords, and foliation are numbered alphabetically and treated as an adjunct to the preceding line of text (as in line 1565a). Interlineations of words or full lines are enclosed within angled lines (thus line 828 \vppon/), but interlined letters are not: all interlineations are recorded in the textual notes. These also record carets, none of which has been printed in the text itself. The position of elements in the text such as speech-prefixes, stage-directions, headings, and indentations is reproduced as exactly as type permits, but other features are normalized. The contents of the additional leaf (Fol. 78+) have been moved to where they should come in the play, interrupting the text on Fol. 44b: the lines the leaf contains have been included sequentially in the play's line numbering.

Scribes have their habits, and the main copyist of Harley MS 7650 is no exception. From an editorial point of view, his most distinctive practice is the use of a symbol closely resembling the comma: this often serves the function of a short virgule, for example, to signify a stop. This mark has been consistently rendered as a comma; the fully fledged virgule is represented as '/'. The scribe was particularly fond of writing the indefinite article 'a' and its following noun without lifting his pen (thus 'astranger' at 104); this, and other, marked irregularities in word divisions are recorded separately at the end of the introduction. Apostrophes are printed even where they appear to be superfluous, and regularized where they are needed but appear to have been misplaced (so 'o'the' at 1704 instead of 'ot'he' as written). The position of punctuation above or below the line has been normalized. Superscript letters have been printed the same size as the remainder of the text. The position of punctuation in abbreviated titles ('M^{r}.', 'S^{r}.') has been regularized. The abbreviations for *per/par* have been expanded, and reproduced in the text in italic (thus line 698 'p*er*ceaue'). Other contractions and tyldes are printed as they appear in the manuscript. Long *s* has been lowered. Capitalization has, necessarily, been more of a matter for editorial judgement but, in line with what appears to be the main scribe's practice, open-stemmed *p*, or deeply cupped *y* and *w* have been treated as upper-case in those instances where a slightly larger letter-form coincides with their occurrence in initial position (especially in proper nouns). Alterations in black ink have been signalled in the textual apparatus by an asterisk.

No attempt has been made in this edition to collate the manuscript with The Hague and London texts of 1649: this must await a full critical edition of the play. However, among the many hundreds of verbal variants, several stage-directions and speech-prefixes in the printed texts supplement and sometimes help to make sense of the play's action as it is recorded in the manuscript. These include a number of asides added at the ends of lines (lines 402, 730, 748, 845, 1376, 1904, 2492) and the slight repositioning and amplification of various entrances and exits. Some speeches are reassigned: from her sister to Lady Huntlove (line 680); from Courtwell to Captain Underwit (line 1669, 'what, what's the matter'); from Sir Francis to Master Courtwell (line 2620); and, incorrectly, from Sir Richard Huntlove to Lady Huntlove (line 750). More valuably, the print supplies a speech-prefix, which has been omitted in the manuscript, for Captain Underwit in line 1298.

The pages in the Plates have been reproduced four fifths full size.

In the preparation of the present edition Anthony Johnson is grateful for the support of Sarah Bannock; and for the advice, on individual matters, of Nigel Bawcutt, Hilton Kelliher, John Pitcher, and Ruby Reid Thompson; and to the Donner Foundation at Åbo Akademi University for generously funding a number of visits to England.

Words undivided in the manuscript which are divided in this edition:

9 a Captaine
12 a Captaine
51 a Buff
a paire
53 a paire
60 a band
75 a leaden
77 a leading
104 a stranger
111 a horse
115 a sconce
129 Countenance, it
162 a Christian
187 a Child
194 a former
201 a Captaine
227 a Comander
232 a pum̃ell
234 a perfect
265 a Noble
273 a scruple
282 knowing by
290 a pretty
293 a purpose
295 a profest
315 a song
318 a Ballet
380 a nearer
387 a Noble
401 but she
402 a confirm'd
414 a thought
430 a seruant
436 a Mast
480 a Letter
568 a Nutt
616 a kind
646 a Coxcombe
690 a pale
734 a pentameter
741 but here
762 a face
819 a passion
853 per la
867 be at
868 a Iudge
959 you Sir
966 throw him
996 a brace
1081 I heard
1114 make hast
1130 a Lute
1274 a knock
1293 a Captaine
1313 a Caualliers
1319 to th'
1379 a stranger
1448 to th'
1464 a plott
1478 a Louer
1497 a spring
a key
1498 his teeth
1532 I hate
1736 a seeming
1851 a licence
1880 a Matrimony
1903 a Clock
1907 de blason
1941 a heathen
1943 a footman
1963 a fresh
1976 a Light
2027 a hollow
2037 a kind
2047 at the
2113 a life
2114 a Sacrifice
2125 a henns
2128 a hand
2197 a Man
2335 a Chamber
2339 a beast
2389 a fall
2414 a footman
2435 vse her
2525 a Lay
2552 a Ladie
2666 a knights
2722 a Ladie
2732 a knights

Words divided in the manuscript which are not divided in this edition:

211	to day
218	a bout
292	to night
	to morrow
486	a bout
563	be tweene
901	to morrow
985	pre the
1003	a bed
1019	a like
1026	A way
1086	a sleepe
1093	a sleepe
1135	a way
1328	a way
1393	a way
1453	to night
1852	a broad
2021	to morrow
2038	a sleepe
2050	a sleepe
2054	a sleepe
2310	a long
2316	to night
2409	a foote
2543	be hind
2576	to night
2635	some thing
2677	a way
2702	a way
2729	to night

List of Characters

This list is based on that given in the quarto of 1649.

SIR RICHARD HUNTLOVE
SIR FRANCIS COURTWELL
MASTER COURTWELL, his Kinsman
MONSIEUR DEVICE
UNDERWIT, a Captain of the Trained Band
SACKBURY, a Captain
ENGINE, a Projector
THOMAS, Servant to Underwit
LADY HUNTLOVE
Her Sister
DOROTHY, a Chambermaid
Servants
Footman
Drawer

you doe not observe the morality of your fancie, nor ye
gentile play and poize of your Lemon, orenge or
or Melon, this is gentry. Why I understand all the
curiosities of the Mode to a Mathematicall point,
and yet I never travaild in all my life for't.
Un: these are extraordinary parts, alas a Captaine has but
fifty or a hundred at most to looke after, and all they
have not so much witt as your french Larquey,
and what need any travaile to instruct them: I can teach
them their motions by word of Mouth, when they come
to fight, my Countrymen will retreate naturally

Enter Ladie and her sister.

La: Now in revenge, could I bee sick, but that
I would not be a prisoner to my Chamber,
these superstitions will make women doe
strange things sometymes.
Sis: Of whome doe you thinke he should be Jealous sister?

PLATE 1: BRITISH LIBRARY, HARL. MS 7650,
FOL. 7b, THE COUNTRY CAPTAIN, LINES 235–51 (HANDS 1 AND 2)

5

La: of Duke Eneas in the hanging –
Sis: I hope he has no suspition of my servants,
that ~~[struck out]~~ under the pretence of formall Courtship
to mee, should ayme at his dishono^r, there's
one that would weare my livery.
La: Device!
hang him outside, no my husband loues ~~his folly~~
his folly, and would haue him the state foole,
his garbes are so ridiculous.
Sis: what opinion,
(still with a confidence of your cleere thoughts)
holdes he of the Knight Sr Francis Courtwell,
that often Visits vs?
La: Sure a Noble one,
if I may aske my Innocence, yet I find
him very amorous O, my husband loues him
he is a powerfull man at Court, whose friendship
is

PLATE 2: FOL. 8a, LINES 252–68 (HANDS 1 AND 2)

I once take leave of those ~~[struck out]~~ celestiall beames
I meet with darkenes in my habitation,
where stretch'd on sable ground, I downe shall lay
my mournefull body, and with folded Armes
heave sadder noats upon ~~then~~ the Irish harpe,
~~and while my footman playes, sigh out my part~~
and drop division with my brimish teares

Sis. this must be lamentable musick sure.

Co. but I have found an Art to cure this wound,
for I with fancies pencill, will so draw
your picture in the table of my hart,
your absence shall but like darke shadowes stand
to sett you of, and see you lady better,
then Love will lett me, when I looke upon you

Sis. Could this be true and meant sweet Sir to me,
I should be kinder then the gentlest spring,
that warmes the world and makes fierce beasts so tame,
and trees to swell themselues to cheerefull greene,
more iocund, then the proudest quire of birds

what

PLATE 3: FOL. 24b, LINES 824–42 (HAND I AND NEWCASTLE'S HAND)

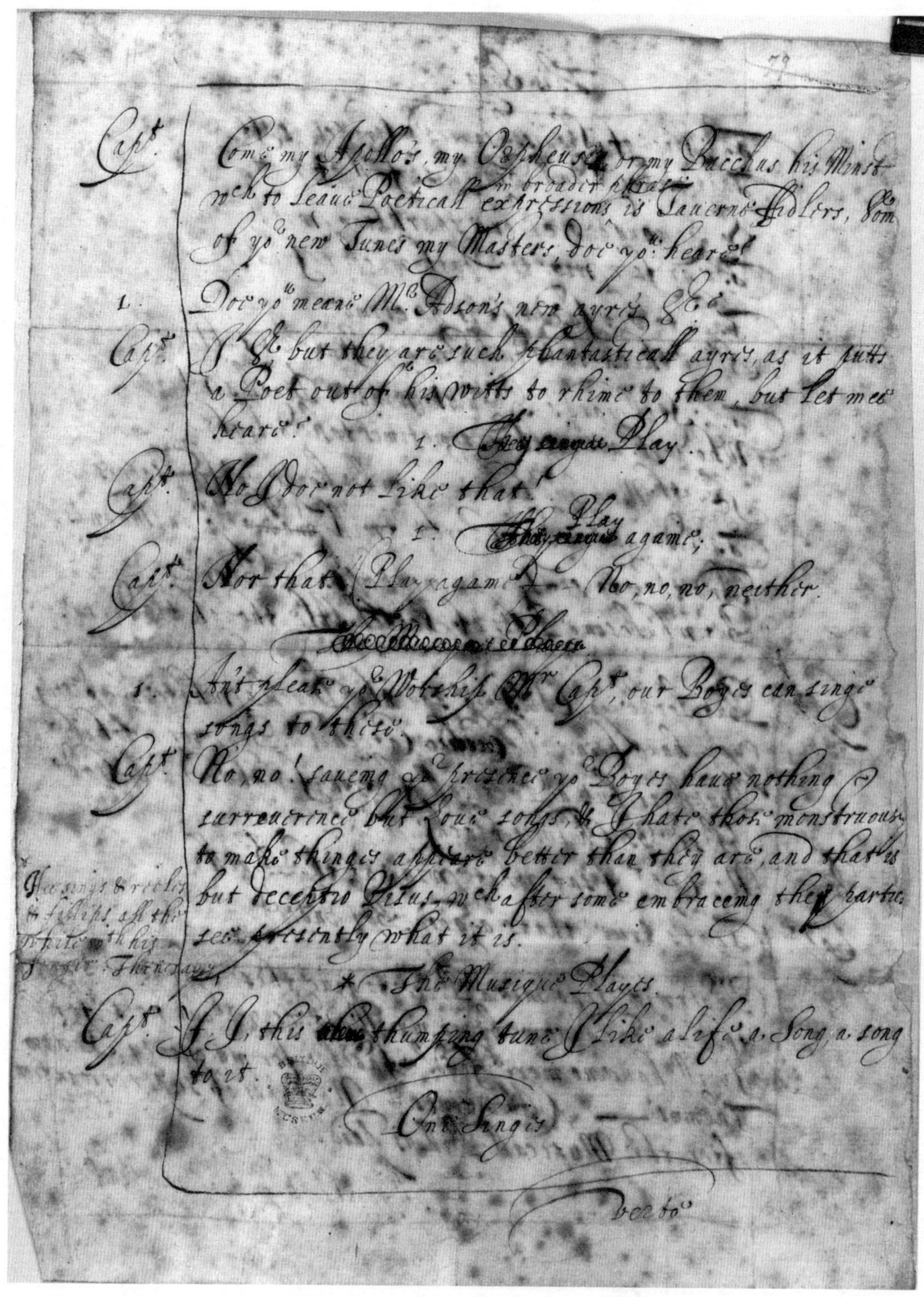

Capt. Come my Apollo's, my Orpheus's, or my Bacchus his Minstr[ells]
wch to leaue Poeticall expressions in broader phrase is Tauerne Fidlers, som
of yor new Tunes my Masters, doe you heare?

1. Doe you meane Mr Adson's new ayres, Sr?

Capt. I Sr but they are such phantasticall ayres, as it putts
a Poet out of his witts to rhime to them, but let mee
heare.

1. They Play.

Capt. No I doe not like that.

1. Play againe.

Capt. Nor that. Play againe. No, no, no, neither.

1. An't please yor Worship Mr Capt., our Boyes can singe
songs to this too.

Capt. No no! sauemg yor presence yor Boyes haue nothing
surreuerence but Loue songs, & I hate those monstruous
to make things appeare better than they are, and that is
but deceptio Visus, wch after some embraceing the partie
see presently what it is.

He sings & reeles & fillips all the while with his finger. Then say[s]

* The Musique Plays.

Capt. I, I, this thumping tune I like aliue: a Song, a song
to it.

One Sings

verto

Plate 4: Fol. 78+a, lines 1517–41a (Rolleston's Hand)

Act the first [Fol. 1a]
Enter Captaine Vnderwit and
his man Thomas.

Vn: Come my man Thomas, and my fathers old man Thomas,
reioyce I say, and triumph, thy Master is honourable,
Tho: then wee are all made,
Vn. No, tis only I am made,
Tho: what and please your worship?
Vn. I am made a Captaine of the traind band Thomas, and
this is my Com̄ission, this very paper hath made me a Captain[e].
Tho: Are you a Paper Captaine Sir? I thought more had gone
to the makeing vp of a Captaine.
Vn: they are fooles that thinke so, Prouided he haue y^{e} fauour of
the Lord Livetenant of the County –
Tho: which it seemes you haue
Vn: the $hono^{r}$ of it, is more, then the thing Thomas, since I
did not bribe the Secrétary, steward, or what servant else
so euer, hath the $gouernm^{t}$ of his $Lo^{p.}$ therein.
Tho: this is very strange, [Fol. 1b]
Vn: Not so much as transitorie wicker bottles to his Deputy
Livetenant, no fewell for his winter, no carriages for
sum̄er, no steple sugar loaues to sweeten his $neighbo^{rs}$
at Christmas, no robbing my leane tennants of their fatt
Capons or Chickins, to present his worship withall Thomas
Tho: I cry your worship mercy, you sold him land the last
terme, I had forgott that.
Vn. I, [and] that lay convenient for him, I vs'd him like a
gentleman, and tooke litle or nothing, 'twere pitty two or
three hundred acres of dirt, shoud make friends fall out, \[wee]/ we
we should haue gone to fenceing schoole.
Tho: how Sir?
Vn. I meane to Westminster hall, and let one anotherd blood in
Lawe
Tho: and so the Land has parted you,
Vn. thou saist right Thomas, it lies betweene both our houses
indeed

lines 4–24 bracketed 5 *triumph*] *h* written over, ? *t* 6 *made,*] , preceded by . 10 *Captain[e]*] *[e]* deleted* 17 *Secrétary*] *c* altered from *r* 20 *transitorie*] ^{1}*i* misformed and not dotted 29 *out,* \\[*wee*]/ *we*] , altered from caret; *[wee]* interlined; *we* obscured in binding 30 *we*] added 31 *Tho*] *o* blotted

indeed, but now I am thus dignified, (I thinke that's a good word), or intituled is better, but tis all one, since I am made a Captaine – [Fol. 2a]

Tho: by your owne desert, and vertue.

Vn. thou art deceaud, it is by vertue of the Com̄ission, the Com= mission is enough to make any man an Officer without desert Thomas, I must thinke how to prouide mee of warlike accoutrements, to accomodate, which comes of Accomodo. Shakespeare the first, and the first

Tho: No Sir it comes of so much money disburs'd.

Vn. in troth and it does Thomas, but take out yor table bookes, and remember to bring after me into the Country, for I will goe downe wth my fatherin law S^{r}. Richard this morning in ye Coach, Let me see, first and formost. A Buff Coate, and a paire of breeches

Tho: first and formost. Item. a Buff Coate for and a paire of breeches of the same Cloth.

Vn. A paire of bootes, and spurres, and a paire of shooes, without Spurres.

Tho: Spurres – [Fol. 2b]

Vn. A paire of gray stockins, thick dapple gray stockins, with a belt, to be worne, either about my shoulder, or about my wast.

Tho: wast.

Vn: a london dutch felt, without a band with a feather in't

Tho: without a feather in't.

Vn. An old fox blade made at Hounsloe heath, and then all the Bookes can be bought of warlike discipline, which the learned call Tacticks.

Tho: Ticktacks – if yor worship would take my Connsell, considering the league at Barwick, and the late ex= peditions wee may find some of these things in the North Or else speake with some reform'd Captaine, though he be a Catholike, and it may bee wee may haue them

36 *dignified*] ^{2}*d* ascender retraced
lines 39–74 bracketed   39 *desert*] *d* bowl altered   40 *Com=*] tylde above *m* deleted   41 *mission*] *m* first and second minims added* to alter it from *i*; ^{1}*i* added*   60 *dutch*] *d* ascender retraced*

at cheaper rates

Vn: tis true Thomas, but I must change the lynings of the
breeches, for I loue to bee cleanly,

Tho. So you may Sir, and haue the fowling of them your selfe, [Fol. 3a]

Vn. Let me see. A leading staff –

Tho: a leaden, staffe –

Vn A leading staffe.

Tho: ding staffe. why a Cane is a leading staffe in a
Captaines hand.

Vn. but I must haue tassells Thomas, and such thinges,

Tho. at the harnesse of the Carthorses, there are tassells, and
Bells too, if you will.

Vn: Bells, what should I doe with em?

Tho. Ring all your companie in.

Vn thou wouldst make me Captaine of a Morris dance,
what serue the Phifes and Drum̄s for, prethee?

Tho. but does yor worship thinke you shall endure the
bouncing of the Gun̄s, I obseru'd you euer kept a
way of, at the Musters.

Vn. thou shalt therefore euery morne goe a birding a=
bout the house, to invre me to the report, by that
tyme thou hast kild all my Pigeons, I shall endure
the noise well enough. /

Tho: but Sir you must haue a dry Nurse, as many Captaines [Fol. 3b]
haue, let me see, I can hire you an old lymping decayed
Sergeant at Brainford, that taught the boyes, he that
had his beard sing'd of, at the last Muster, hee'le doe
it brauely.

Vn: what must he haue?

Tho: alas twenty pipes of Barmudas a day, six flagons of
March beere, a quart of Sack in a weeke, for he
Scornes meate, and the kitchin[g] wench to bring ye shirt
to him, and the only band, for Cuffs he getts none, but
such as his drunkennes procures him with quarrelling

Vn. No, I shall be bashfull to learne of a stranger, thou

lines 79–83 bracketed
line 85 bracketed
lines 86–8 bracketed
lines 93–103 bracketed

84 *wouldst*] *st* added*
85 *prethee?*] *?**
101 *kitchin[g]*] *g* bowl blotted, two lines through tail
103 *procures*] *e* lower loop smudged

shat goe seeke out Captaine Sackburye.
Tho: He that weares no money in his scarlett hose, and when
he is drunke is infected with Connsell?
Vn. the very same, you shall find him at his lodging in
Fleetstreet, or in ye next tauerne, giue him this Letter,
tell him I desire his Companie this summer in ye Country,
he shall haue a horse of mine say, here, giue him this
gold too.
Tho: I hope it is gameing gold. [FOL. 4a]
Vn. he shall read warres to me, and fortification.
Tho: I can teach you to build a sconce Sir.
Vn. beside, he is very valiant, he beate me twice, when he
was drunk, but poore fellow, I ask'd him forgiuenes
the next day. make hast good Thomas, and remember
all the Tacticks.
Tho: I warrant you sir. I know 'em well enough.
Vn. So, so here's Sir Richard Exit

Enter Sir Richard Huntloue, his Ladie
and Mistresse Dorothy

S^{r}. me thinkes [he] \you/ looke[s] more sprightly,
Since you were made a Captaine.
Vn. Oh good S^{r}. Richard, indeed my face is the worst part about
mee, and yet, it will serue at the Muster
Do: Serue? with reverence to the title, I haue seene a
Generall with a worse Countenance, it is a good leading face
and

and though you haue no cut o're the nose, or other [FOL. 4b]
visible scarre, w^{c}h I doubt not, but you may receaue
all in \good/ tyme, it is a quarrelling face, and fitt for a
Man of warre.
Vn. I thanke you sweet mistress Dorothy; I will comēnd you,
as much, when you are in the Conntry; but doe you
resolue to goe downe this morning Sir?
S^{r}. by all meanes: is your sister readie? bid the Coachman
make hast, and haue a care, you leaue none of yor

105 *Sackburye*] *y* first minim blotted and altered; .* 107 *Connsell?*] *?** 109 *tauerne*] additional stop under ^{2}e
113 *gold.*] .* 114 *fortification*] ^{2}f ascender blotted 119 *all*] added, ? Hand 2 121 *Exit*] with box rule
124 *you*] interlined above deletion* *looke[s]* deleted* 125 *made*] *d* ascender retraced 128 *Serue?*] *e* and *?*
written together; *?* preceded by , Hand 1 132 *good*] interlined above caret* 136 *Sir?*] *?** 138 *of*] *f* has otiose
mark

trinketts behind, after a litle dialogue wth my scriueno^{r}
Ile returne, and then to Coach.

La: But why this expedition, this posting out of towne,
as the Aire were infected?

S^{r}. the truth is, my sweet Ladie, wee haue no Exchange in y^{e}
Conntry, no Playes, no Masques, no Lord Maiors day,
no gulls nor gallifoists. Not so many Ladies to Visit,
and weare out my Coach wheeles, no dainty Madams
in

in Childbedd, to set you a longing when you come home, [FOL. 5a]
to lie in, with the same fashion'd Curtaines, and hangings,
such curious siluer Andirons, Cupbord of plate, and
Pictures, you may goe to Church in ye Countrey, without a
new Satten gowne, and play at penny gleeke with a
Iustice of peaces wife, and the Parsons; show yor white
hand, with but one Diamond, when you carue, and not be
asham'd to weare your owne wedding ring with the old
Poesie. There are no Doctors to make you sick wife,
No legends of lies brought home, by yong gallants,
that fill my Dyning roome with fleas, and new fashions,
that will write Verses vpon the handle of yor fanne,
and comend the education of yor Monkey, w^{c}h is so like
their worships, as they were all of one familie. I haue
no humo^{r} to provokeing meates, I will downe, and enter
into a Christian diett Madam, there is sport in killing my
owne Patridge and Pheasant, my Trowtes will cost me less
then yor lobsters and crayfish drest with Amber greece,
and

and I may renew my acquaintance w^{t}h Mutton, and [FOL. 5b]
bold chines of beefe, entertaine my tenants y^{t} would pay
for my housekeeping all the yeere, and thanke my wor^{p}.
at Christmas, ouer and aboue [my] \their/ rents, w^{t}h Turkies
and Beeues of supererogation. You may guesse I haue
some reason to change the aire wife, and so I leaue you
to prepare your selfe. you haue my purpose, and

142 *infected?*] ?* 146a *in*] *i* dotted*, preceded by Hand 1 dot 147 *in*] *i* dotted*, preceding Hand 1 dot lines 148–50 bracketed 148 *fashion'd*] *io* altered, ? from *o* 149 *Cupbord*] *p* altered from *b* 157 *roome*] ^{2}*o* altered, ? from first two minims of *m* 158 *fanne*] *e* head blotted 161 *downe,*] ,* 164 *lobsters*] *e* altered* from *a* 168 *their*] interlined above deletion, ? Hand 1 170 *aire*] *i* added*

may expect mee Exit
La: How euer he pretend, and point at charge,
which makes his stay vnpleasant, tis his Ielousie,
that strikes him into wildnes, and dislike
of all things here, he does not vse mee well,
Where is my sister?
Do: In the Closet Madam.
I must waite vpon my Ladie sweete Captaine
Ex.
Vn: this wench has a notable witt, if I haue any Iudgment.
I doe not thinke but shee's in loue with me, if I thought
shee were not giuen to be with child, I would examine
her.
her abilities, but these waiting women are so fruitfull, [Fol. 6a]
when they haue a good turne from a gentleman, they
haue not the vertue of concealement, touch a Chamber=
maide, and take a Child, euery thing workes with their
soluble bodies.
Enter Mounsir Device [and his man].
De. Noble M^{r}. Vnderwitt!
Vn: I know not whome you meane Sir, he that comands the
family in Chiefe, hath been honor'd with a sword, and
rise Sir Richard, (who is but my fatherinlawe to a
[fo] by a former wife), for M^{r}. Vnderwitt, whome to salute
you humbled yor Cloth a gold Dublet, I ken not the wight,
De. Doe not you know mee Noble Sir?
Vn: Vpon euen tearmes I may call your name to memorie,
but if you vnderstand not my addition, it is honourable
to forgett the best friend I haue.
De. What's the mistery of this? yor addition, pray hono^{r} me to know it
Vn: he that was M^{r}. Vnderwit is made a Captaine, you may [Fol. 6b]
if you please, take notice of his title.
De: I begg your mercy noble Captaine, and Congratulate yor
addition of hono^{r}, It was Ignorance, which I professe, made
me salute you with a wrong preface, & Now, Capt. I shall bee

173 *pretend,*] ,* *charge,*] ,* 180 *Ex.*] .*, preceded by Hand 1. 189 *[and his man]*] hatched over*
190 *Vnderwitt!*] !* 196 *Sir?*] ?* 200 *this?*] ?* 205 *&* . . . *Capt.*] *&* added*; *t.* altered, ? Hand 1

proud to march vnder the ensigne of your fauour.
Vn: friend Device how does thy body? I am thy
Vassall, Seruant is for porters, watermen, & lackquies & is no
witt neither. /
you preserue yor tropes and yor elegancies what fancies
doe adorne today, if I were a Constable I might apprehend
you for suspition you had robd a Pedlar,
does this thatchd Cottage head hold still in fashion?
what paid you for this deadmans haire? where's
yor night raile, the last tyme I see you was in
a shopp in Fleetstreet, where at Complement
and bare to an other gentleman I tooke him for a Barber, and
I

I thought you by the wide lynnen about your neck, haue [Fol. 7a]
been vnder correction in the suds Sir.
De: Wee are gouern'd by the Mode; as waters by the Moone,
but there are more changes in [th] one then t'other, but
does your Comand extend to the Sea, or the land
Service?
Vn: I neuer see the Sea in my life Sir, nor intend it.
De. You are not the first Captaine, that has seene no service,
tis tyme lost to travell for't, when a Man may bee
a Comander at home. I neuer traveld my selfe.
Vn. No Sir?
De. and yet I vnderstand garbes, from the eleuation
of your Pole, to the most humble galosh,
Vn. Can your hanches play well in these close cut breeches?
they want but a pum̄ell to distinguish 'em from
Trouses.
De: O Sir, there is a perfect Geometry in these breeches,
you

you doe not obserue, the morality of your fancie, nor y^{e} [Fol. 7b]
gentile play and [posture] \poize/ of your Lemon, Orenge or
or Melon, this is gent[⟨.⟩]y. Why I vnderstand all the

lines 207–9, bracketed 207 *body?*] ?* 209 *witt*] *i* dotted* *neither. /*] . marked twice
line 210 (*what fancies*) underlined
lines 212–17 bracketed 212 *Pedlar,*] ,* 213 *fashion?*] ?* preceded by ., ? Hand 1 214 *haire?*] ?*
216 *Fleetstreet,*] ,*
lines 218–19 bracketed 218 *neck,*] ,* 219 *Sir.*] .* above ., Hand 1 220 *Mode;*] blot above ;
222 *Sea,*] ,* 223 *Service?*] ?* 224 *it.*] .* 225 *are*] *r* blotted *service,*] ,* 226 *for't*] '*
227 *selfe.*] .* 228 *Sir?*] ?*
lines 231–2 bracketed 231 *breeches?*] ?* 233 *Trouses*] *u* altered 236 *[posture]*] hatched over* *poize*]
interlined above deletion*, Hand 2 237 *gent[⟨.⟩]y*] ⟨.⟩ probably *r*, deleted*; .* *vnderstand*] *v* altered

[punct⟨.⟩ualities] \curiosities/ of the Mode to a Mathematicall point,
and yet I neuer trauaild in all my life for't.
Vn: these are extraordinary parts, alas a Captaine, has but
fifty or a hundred at most to looke after, and all they
haue not so much witt as your french Lacquey. /
and what need any travaile to instruct them? I can teach
them their motions by word of Mouth, when they come
to fight, my Countrymen will retreate naturally
Enter Ladie and hir sister. /
La: Now in revenge, could I bee sick, but that
I would not be a Prisoner to my Chamber,
these superstitions will make Women doe
strange things sometymes.
Sis: Of whome doe you thinke he should be Iealous sister?
La: of Duke Eneas in the hanging – [Fol. 8a]
Sis: I hope he has no suspition of my servants,
that [made] \vnder/ the pretence of formall Courtship
to mee, should ayme at his dishono^{r}, there's
one that would weare my livery.
La: Device?
hang him outside, no my husband loues [his folly]
his folly, and would haue him the State foole,
his garbes are so ridiculous.
Sis: what opinion,
(still with a confidence of your cleere thoughts)
holdes he of the Knight S^{r}. Francis Courtwell,
that often visits vs?
La: Sure a Noble one,
if I may aske my Innocence, yet I find
him very amorous O, my husband loues him
he is a powerfull man at Court, whose freindship
is
is worth preserveing Sister, I confesse [Fol. 8b]
his noblenesse, and person, hath prevaild
with mee, to giue him still the freest welcome
my modestie, and honor would permitt,

238 *[punct⟨.⟩ualities]*] hatched over* *curiosities*] interlined above deletion*, Hand 2 *point,*] ,* 239 *for't*] '* 243 *travaile*] *v* altered *instruct*] *s* altered from *t*, Hand 1 *them?*] ?* added over , line 245 (*to fight, my Countrymen*) bracketed 251 *sister?*] ?* 252 *hanging* –] –* 254 *[made]*] hatched over* *vnder*] interlined above deletion*, Hand 2 256 *livery*.] .* 257 *Device?*] ?* 258 *[his folly]*] single-stroke deletion, ? Hand 1 259 *the State foole*] *he State foole* added* 270 *noblenesse*] *ne* interlined above caret; *se* added*

but if I thought, my husband had a scruple
his Visits were not honourable, I
should soone declare how much I wish his absence.
Vn. Your Mistresse, and my Lady. I haue some
affaires require dispatch, ile leaue you to 'em.
Exit
Sis. My witty servant
La: Most pretious Alamode Monsir De=vice.
De: I blesse my lipps with yor white handes,
La: you come to take your leaue, as knowing by
instinct, wee haue but halfe an houre to stay
Sis. Wee are for the Countrey as fast as y^{e} flanders Mares
will trott sir
De. that's a Solecisme, till the Court remove, are you afraide [Fol. 9a]
of the small Pox?
Sis: the less the better for a gentlewoman,
De. and the greater more genty for a Cauallier,
by this gloue, (a pretty embroidery ist not)? you must
not depriue Vs so soone of your sweet presence[?]
Why there's a Ball tonight in the Strand, and tomorrow
I had a purpose to waite vpon you to ye pictures, I ha'
bespoke regalias there too, there will be a new play
shortly, a Pretty Comedy written by a profest Scholler
he scornes to take money for his witt as the
Poets doe
La: he is Charitable to the Actors
Sis. It may be their repentance enough to play it.
De: You must needs stay, and giue your opinion,
what will become of me when you are gone Ladie?
La: if your devotion catch not cold, you may breath yor Barbary
and visit vs, where you may be confident of yor welcome,
De I dare as soone doubt I was Christned. but pray let vs [Fol. 9b]
visit the Exchange, and take a trifle to weare for my
sake, before you goe. What say Madam? my owne Coach
is at doore, the lyning is very rich, and the horses

276 *Lady.*] .* 280 *Monsir De=vice.*] added* 283 *instinct*] ^{2}*i* blotted 286 *are*] *r* altered 291 *[?]* deleted by two vertical strokes, the second possibly * 294 *regalias*] ^{2}*a* altered from *u* 299 *it.*] .* 300 *opinion,*] ,* 301 *Ladie?*] ?* 306 *Madam?*] ?*, ? Hand 1; ? written above ,

are very well matcht.
La: alas wee expect vpon my husbands returne, to take Coach
im̄ediatlie
Sis. but if wee may see you in the Countrey, you will doe
vs an hono^{r}.
De: You invite me to my happines, I can play well
o'the kittar, I thinke your musique is but course there
wee'le haue a Conntry dance after supper, and a song
I can talke loud to a Theorbo too, and that's cald singing
Now, yee shall heare my Ballet.
Sis: Did you make a Ballet?
De: Oh I, the greatest wit lies that way now, a pittifull
Complaint of the Ladies, when they were banish'd
the Towne with their husbands to their Countrey houses, [FOL. 10a]
compeld to change the deere delight of Maske and Revells,
here, for Wassall, and windie bagpipes, instead of Silken Fairies
tripping in the Banquetting Roome, to see the Clownes sell fish
in the hall, and ride the wild Mare, and such Olimpicks; till the
ploughman breake his Crupper, at which the villagers and
plumporidge men boile ouer, while the Dairy maid laments
the defect of his Chine, and he poore man disabled for
the trick, endeauo^{r} to stifle the noise, and company with
[such] perfume of sweat instead of Rose water.
La: this must be our Countrey recreation too.
Enter S^{r}. Francis Courtwell
De: who is this?
La: tis S^{r}. Francis Courtwell.
you cannot chose but know him; this must bee
a fauour Sir to Visit vs at parting.
Fr: I came with other expectation Madam,
then
then to heare this, I could receaue no newes [FOL. 10b]
so vnwelcome, what misfortune doth conclude
the Towne so vnhappie?
la: tis my husbands pleasure,

308 *matcht.*] .* 312 *hono^{r}.*] .*
lines 313–19 (*now,*) bracketed; bracket extended to 320 313 *happines*] *i* dotted* 318 *Ballet?*] ?*
lines 320–6 bracketed 322 *deere*] ^{1}*e* altered from *r* 323 *instead*] *a* bowl misformed 325 *Olimpicks;*] ; altered* from , 330 *[such]*] hatched over* *water.*] .* 331 *too.*] .* 334 *Courtwell.*] .* 335 *chose*] *o* altered 340 *vnhappie?*] ?*

affrighted with some Dreame he had last night,
for I can guess no other cause.

Fr: could hee
bee capeable of fright, and you so neere him?

De. he cannot choose but know me then. S^{r}. I kisse your
Noble hand, and shall be stellified in your knowledge

Fr. what thing's this, that looke so like a race Nagg trick'd
with ribbands?

Sis. he is one of my inamoratos sir, they call [him]
him Mounsir De-vice.

Fr: Lady your faire excuse – he has it seemes
some confidence to preuaile vpon your liking,
that he hath bought so many Bride laces.

Sis. You may interpret him a walking mirth, [Fol. 11a]

Fr: he moues vpon some skrue, and may be kinsman
to the engine, that is drawne about with Cakebread,
but that his outside's brighter.

De: S^{r}. Francis Courtwell.

Fr: that's my name sir?

De. and myne Mounsieur device.

Fr. A frenchman Sir?

De. No sir an English Monsier, made vp by a Scotch
taylor that was Prentice in France, I shall
write my greatest ambition satisfied, if you
please to lay your Comands vpon mee.

Fr: Sweet lady, I beseech you mussell yor beagle, I dare
not trust my selfe with his folly, and he may
deserue more beating, then I am willing to bestow at
this tyme.

Sis. take truce a little seruant.

Fr: will you consider Madam yet, how much [Fol. 11b]
a wounded hart may suffer?

La: Still the old businesse,
indeed you make me blush, but I forgiue you,
if you will promise to sollicite this

347 *hand,*] mark like a 7 below *d* and above , 350 *inamoratos*] ^{2}*o* altered from *e* *[him]*] double-stroke deletion; *h* altered 351 *De-vice.*] - and . added* 354 *laces.*] .* 358 *outside's*] *o* altered 361 *device*] *c* altered from *n* 362 *Sir?*] ?*

lines 363–4 bracketed 366 *mee.*] .* preceded by ., Hand 1 367 *dare*] *d* ascender retraced 370 *tyme.*] *e* blotted; .* preceded by ., Hand 1 373 *suffer?*] ?* 375 *indeed*] ^{1}*d* and ^{2}*d* retraced

vnwelcome cause no [longer] more.
Fr: tis my desire,
I take no pleasure in a pilgrimage,
if you instruct [in] a nearer way, tis in
Your will to saue your Eare the trouble of
my Pleading Madam; if with one soft breath
You say I'me entertain'd, but For one smile
that speakes consent, you'le make my life yor seruant.
La. My husband sir –
Fra: Deserues not such a treasure to himselfe
and sterue a Noble seruant.
La: you but pleade [FOL. 12a]
for vanitie, desist, for if I could
(forgetting hono^{r} and my modestie)
allow your wild desires, it were impossible
that wee should meete, more then in thought, and shadowes.
Fr: if those shadowes madam be but darke enough,
I shall accompt it happines to meet you.
but referr that to opportunitie, which our
kind starrs in Pitty will sooner offer
to both our ioyes
La: but he is very Iealous.
Fr: that word assures my victorie, I neuer
I [neuer] heard any wife accuse her husband, of
or cold neglect, or Iealousie, but she had
a confirm'd thought within, to trick his forehead.
It is but Iustice Madam to reward him
for his suspitious thoughts.
La. d'ee thinke it fitt [FOL. 12b]
to punish his suspition, yet perswade to Act the
Sinne he feares?
Fr. Custome, and nature make it less offence
in women, to comitt the deed of pleasure,
then men to doubt their chastities, this, flowing
from poison'd natures, that excus'd by frailty.

377 *[longer]*] triple-stroke deletion *more.*] .* 384 *seruant.*] .* 386 *Deserues*] *D* ascender blotted 389 *desist*] *d* bowl altered from *s* 392 *shadowes.*] .* 394 *you.*] .* 398 *Iealous.*] .* 400 *[I neuer]*] hatched over* 402 *forehead.*] .* 407 *feares?*] ?* 411 *frailty.*] .*

yet I haue heard the way to cure the feare,
has bin the deed, at truth the scruples vanish,
I speake not Madam, with a thought, to suffer
a foule breath whisper your white name, for he
that dares traduce it, must beleeue me dead,
or my fame twisted with your honour, must not
haue pitty on the Accusers blood.

De: I will attend you in the Countrey, [and] I
take my leaue and kiss your Iuory hand,
Madam and yours. S^r. Francis your obliged.
exit.

Fr: you bless me with this promise, [FOL. 13a]
how can you lady suffer this impertinent
afflict you thus? ex. lad.

Sis. Alas my Parrat's dead, and he supplies the prattle
i'th spring and fall, he will saue me charge of phisick
in purgeing Melancholy.

Fr. If you dare
accept a seruant Ladie, vpon my
comends, I should present a kinsman t'ee,
who shanot want \a/ fortune, nor I hope
a meritt, to possesse your faire opinion.

Sis. You doe not say he is hansome all this while,
and that's a maine consideration, I wod not haue
a man so tall as a Mast, that I must clyme the
shroudes to kisse him, nor so much a dwarfe,
that I must vse a multiplying glass, to know
the proportion of his limbes, a great man is
a
a great house with too much garret, and his [FOL. 13b]
head full of nothing but lumber, if he be too round
agen, hee's only fitt to bee hung vpp in a
[Chri] Cristall glasse. The truth is, the man I loue,
must please me at first sight, if he take my eye,
I may take more tyme to examine his talent.

418 *blood.*] .* 419 *[and]*] hatched over 422 *exit.*] added* 423 *Fr:*] blotted 425 *thus?*] ?* *ex. lad.*] *, possibly Hand 2 432 *a*] interlined above caret 433 *opinion.*] .* lines 440–1 (*lumber,*) bracketed 442 *agen,*] ,*

Fr. do you but grace him with accesse, and aske your
owne fancie, ladie, how you can affect him.
Ile not despaire if he were cur'd of modesty,
which is the whole fault in his behauiour,
but he may passe without contempt.
Do: that modestie is a foule fault.

Enter Captaine Vnderwitt

Vn: Come away Cosen, S^{r}. Richard's come and calls for you
the Coachman is ready to Mount, Noble S^{r}. Francis
because you may not loose breath you may call me a Capt.
and please you \a Captaine/ o'the traind band.
Sis: tis very certaine. [FOL. 14a]
Fr: I congratulate your title Sir.
Vn: if you come into the Countrey, you shall see me doe
as much with my leading staff, as an other.
Fr. you wonot thrash your men.
Vn. if I did, tis not the first tyme I ha thrash'd, if I
find my Souldiers tractable, they shall find me but a
reasonable Captaine.

Enter Sr Richard. Lady

S^{r}. Sir Francis I am sorrie the violence of my affaires
wonot let me entertaine you to my wishes, pray hono^{r}
vs with your presence in the Countrey, if you can
dispence with your employment, where, I shall satisfie
for this hast of my departure.
S^{r}. Fr: I shall attend you Sir, and present a kinsman of mine
to this virgin Ladie, he is like to be Master of no narrow fortune,
it was my busines at this tyme, \only/ to prepare his accesse.
S^{r}. He shall haue my vote for your sake S^{r}. Francis, come
madam. [FOL. 14b]
Fr: Ile waite vpon you to the Coach, and take my leaue
Vn: Sweet Mistresse Doritye. / Ex^{t}.

Act the second.

Enter Captaine Sackurie reading
a Letter and Thomas. /

447 *him.*] .* 450 *contempt.*] .*, preceded by ., Hand 1 456 *a Captaine*] interlined above caret*, Hand 2 457 *certaine.*] .* 458 *Sir.*] .* 461 *men.*] .* 464 *Captaine.*] .* 470 *departure.*] .* 473 *it*] *i* dotted* *only*] interlined*, ? Hand 2 *accesse.*] .* 478 *second*] *c* altered from *o*

Cap: hum – hum – where's the gold?
Tho: here Sir, one, two, three, fower, and five,
Cap: thou hast learnd the Cinque pace Tho:, is the gold weight?
Tho: I hope so Sir.
Cap: hum – into the Countrey, – thou hast a horse too.
Tho: Not about me Sir, but he is ready all but brideling and
sadling at our Inne Captaine, my Master sayes, you shalbe
troubled with no horse but his,
Cap: why is he lame?
Tho: what Truehunt, the black nag, with three white feete? he [Fol. 15a]
lame? you meane, that, I ride vpon my selfe.
Cap: hum – make hast, as you will preserue the reputation
of your true friend and seruant. – so so –
comend me to him, Thomas, I wonot faile to visit him.
Tho. You may demand the Nag, if you aske for Humfrey the
Ostler, by the same token, he has bin there this foure dayes,
and had but one Peck of Prouender.
Cap: Enough I wonot faile I say. Farwell, honest Tom
a Lincolne, farewell, comend me to the traind band.
Tho: Pray doe not fall a drinking, and forgett it
bu'oy Noble Captaine. Exit

Enter Mr. Courtwell.

Cap: My expectation of the Law, well mett,
Cou: I am glad to see you Captaine,
Cap. is thy sight perfect?
thy poring vpon statutes, and booke Cases
makes
makes me suspect, but dost thou thinke to bee [Fol. 15b]
a Dominus fac totum on the Bench,
and be a Ciuill Lawyer?
Cou: you are merry.
Cap. tis more, then thou hast been this tweluemonth, th'ast
lost thy Complexion with too much study.
why thou shalt be an heire, and rule the rost
of halfe a shire, and thy father would but dye once,

483 *weight?*] ?* 484 *Sir.*] .* 485 *Countrey, –*] –* added over , *too.*] .* 487 *sayes,*] ,* 488 *his,*] ,* 490 Fol. 15a] 5 altered from 4 *feete?*] ?*, added over , 491 *selfe.*] .* 494 *him.*] .* 497 *Prouender.*] .* 501 *Captaine.*] .* 505 *perfect?*] ?* 509 *Lawyer?*] ?* 510 *are*] *e* added* 511 *more,*] ,* 512 *study.*] . marked twice

Come to the Sizes with a band of Ianisaries,
to equall the grand Signior, all thy tenants;
that shall at their owne charge make themselues fine,
and march like Caualiers with tilting feathers,
gaudy, as Agamemnons in the play,
after whome, thou like St George ahorseback,
or the high Sheriffe, shall make the Countrey people
fall downe, in adoration of thy Crooper,
and Siluer strirrup my right worshipfull.
A

a Pox a buckram, and the baggage in't, [FOL. 16a]
Papers defil'd with Court hand, and long dashes,
Or Secretarie lines that stradle more
then Frenchmen, and lesse wholsome to the Client,
is thy head to be fild with Proclamations,
reioynders, and hard words beyond the Alchemist?
be ruld, and liue like a fine gentleman,
that may haue haukes, and hounds, & whores, & horses,
and then thou art fitt Companie.

Cou: You talke wildlie,
I wou'd you saw your Erro^{r}, that place all
your happinesse vpon such course delights,
I should degenerate too much, and forfet
my education.

Cap. Education, he has gott a tune.
I doe not thinke but thou wilt leaue thy law,
and exercise thy talent in composeing
some

some treatises against long haire, and drinking [FOL. 16b]
that most vnchristian weed yclipt tobacco,
Preach to the Puisnes of the Inne sobrietie,
and abstinence from shaueing of lewd Baylies,
that will come shortlie to your Chamber doores,
and there with reverence, entreat yor worships

515 *Ianisaries*] ^{1}*a* altered from *e* 516 *tenants;*] ; altered* from , 517 *fine,*] ,* 518 *feathers,*] ,* 520 *whome,*] ,* *ahorseback,*] ,* 522 *downe,*] ,* *Crooper,*] ,* 523 *worshipfull.*] .* Fol. 16a] *6* altered from *5* 524 *baggage*] ^{2}*a* blotted 525 *hand,*] ,*, preceded by Hand 1 , 528 *Proclamations*] *i* altered from *e* 536 *degenerate*] ^{3}*e* altered* *forfet*] ^{2}*f* altered* from *g* 537 *education.*] .* 538 *tune.*] .* 540 *composeing*] *osein* altered* from *arein* 542 *tobacco*] *b* altered 543 *Inne*] *e* altered* from *s* 544 *Baylies,*] ,*

come forth, and be arrested. precious tappoles!
I wo'd not willinglie despaire of thee
for thy Lands sake, and cause I am thy Countryman,
One generous Vagarie, and thou wer't wise,
would breake somebodies hart, within a señight,
and then th'art Lord of all, haue but the grace
to dine wo'mee at tauerne, and ile tell
thy friends there is some hope.
Cou: My friendes?
Cap: thy father's
in Essex, if he liue heele purchase Romford,
if
if he die sooner, then the towne's our owne. [FOL. 17a]
Spend but an Acre a day, and thou maist live,
till all the world be wearie of thee, betweene
vs two, what thinke you of a wench?
Cou: Nothing.
Cap: You meane, one wench betweene vs two, is nothing.
I know a hundred leuerets, things that will
bound like a dancer on the rope, and kiss thee
into thy naturall complexion,
a Sinner, that shall clime thee like a squirrell,
Cou: and crack me like a Nutt, I ha no kernell
to spare for her sweet tooth.
Cap: that was a metaphor, hee's not desperate.
Cou: buoy my deere Captaine
Cap: Wy farewell Countreyman,
I may liue yett to witnes thy conversion
Exit
Enter a footeman [FOL. 17b]
Cou. How does my vncle
Io: he desires presentlie
to speake with you at his lodging
Cou. Ile attend him. Ex^{t}
Enter Captaine [Spruce] \vnderwitt/ and Thomas.
Vn. and hast thou been carefull of all those things I gaue

547 *arrested.*] .* *tappoles!*] !* 549 *Countryman,*] ,* 550 *wise,*] ,* 551 *señight,*] ,* 552 *all,*] ,* 553 *wo'mee*] *m* altered*, with blot above; ^{2}e added* 554 *hope.*] .* 557 *Essex,*] ^{1}s altered from *x*; ,* *Romford,*] , preceded by . 558 *owne.*] .* 562 *Cou:*] *C* top flourished 563 *nothing.*] .* 570 *desperate.*] .* 572 *Countreyman,*] ,* 580 *[Spruce]*] hatched over *vnderwitt*] interlined above deletion

Charge to be prouided?
Tho: there is a note of the particulars.
Vn: tis very well done Thomas – let me see Imprimis –
Tho. the Captaine wonot faile to be w'ee sir, he was not at his
lodging, and enquiring at the horne tauerne, I heard he
had been there with two or three Cittizens y^{t} ow'd him mony
Vn: that he owde money to.
Tho: tis all one I thinke Sir. for when Captaines haue not [pay]
pay, the creditors may pay themselues, here they said, he
did mollifie the hart of the haberdashers, & dranke him
selfe
selfe a litle mellowe ere they parted, wch gaue me some [Fol. 18a]
hope, I might find him ere night at the Diuell, where
indeed I fetcht him out of the fire, and gaue him yor
Letter. /
Vn. and the gold too?
Tho: that was the first word he read, if you did not write
it in text, he could not haue found it out so soone. his
eye was no sooner in the inside? but his arme flew out, wth
an open mouth, and his very fingers cryed, giue me the gold, w^{ch}
presumeing to be wieght, he put into his hocas pocas, a
litle dormer vnder his right skirt, and so takeing his word
to come downe, and turning ouer your horse to him, with
Caution, not to be drunk, and forgett your wo^{p}; I tooke my
leaue, and went about my Inventorie.
Vn: theis things are very right Thomas – let me see [more] now,
the bookes of Martiall discipline.
Tho: I bought vp all, that I found haue relation to warr, and fighting. [Fol. 18b]
Vn: that was weldonne – Item. the sword Salue.
Tho: this I conceiu'd, to haue the vertue of Achilles speare,
if you bee hurt, you need goe no further, then ye blade for a
Surgeon.
Vn: the Buckler of faith.
Tho: you had the sword before sir.
Vn: A booke of mortification.

582 *prouided?*] ?* 583 *particulars.*] .* 584 *Vn:*] *V* misformed 585 *sir,*] ,* 588 *to.*] .* 589 *Sir.*] .* *[pay]*] single-stroke deletion 590 *themselues,*] ,* *said,*] ,* 594 *fire*] *i* dotted*, preceding Hand 1 dot *him*] *i* dotted*, preceding Hand 1 dot 596 *too?*] ?* 599 *inside*] ^{1}*i* dotted*; ^{2}*i* dotted*, preceding Hand 1 dot *his*] *i* dotted*, preceding Hand 1 dot *arme*] *r* altered* 600 *an*] added* *mouth*] *u* retraced* 602 *takeing*] *a* altered 606 *[more]*] single-stroke deletion 609 *weldonne*] altered* from *welcome* 611 *for*] *f* downstroke retraced* 615 *mortification*] *at* altered*; ^{3}*i* dotted*; *o* altered*

Tho. I Sir, that is a kind of killing, which I thought very necessary
for a Captaine.
Vn. Item the gunpowder treason, and the Booke of Cannons.
Tho: I wod not lett [any or all] \any/ shott scape mee.
Vn: Shakespeares workes – why Shakespeares workes?
Tho: I had nothing for the pikemen before,
Vn: they are Playes,
Tho. Are not all your musterings in the Countrey, so, sir? pray read on
Vn: Bellarmines Controuersie in six tomes.
Tho: that I tooke vpon the Stationers word, who had been a pretty [FOL. 19a]
Schollar at Paules, for the word Bellarmine he said, did comprehend
warr, weapons and wordes of defiance, ill wordes prouoke men to \draw/
their sword, and fighting makes an end of the busines, and all
this is controversy, Pray goe on sir.
Vn: two paire of Tables. tables for what?
Tho: Oh Sir for ticktack. you know it was in my note, which though I
doubted at first, yet considering you were newly made a Cap; I
I conceiv'd it was fitt you should learne to sett, and orer your men.
Vn: tacticks man, thou didst mistake, they are bookes of warre.
Tho: you cannot know these from bookes, as they are painted, I warrant you.
Vn: why dost thou thinke theis will make a Souldier?
Tho: Not of themselues sir, and therefore I prouided; please you read on Sir
Vn: Parsons Resolutions, and Felthams resolues.
Tho: All is nothing I knew Sir without resolution.
Vn: Sum̄a totalis three and twenty poundes Nyneteene shillings and Seuen
pence, thou hast vndone mee. /
Tho. if you doe not like the pennyworths tis but the charges of my selfe [FOL. 19b]
and a horse agen to London, I will loose but the three odd pounds
19^{s} and 7^{d}., it may be, you doe not vnderstand these Authors, when
the Captaine comes, he will expound 'em to you
Vn What a Coxcombe haue I to my man? but I dare not be angry with
him, well carry 'em into my study Thomas. Ext. Tho:

Enter [Engine and his page] \Device/

De: Most honor'd Captaine.
Vn My compleat Mon̄sier Device, this is a grace to vs

616 *killing*] [1]*i* dotted* 617 *Captaine.*] ., preceded by Hand 1, 618 *gunpowder*] *r* altered from partly erased *d*, probably Hand 1 619 *[any or all]*] hatched over* *any*] interlined above deletion* 620 *workes?*] ?* 623 *sir?*] ?* above , 624 *tomes.*] .*, preceding Hand 1 . 625 *that*] [2]*t* followed by blot 627 *draw*] interlined above caret 629 *sir.*] .*, preceded by . 632 *I*] partly cropped 633 *I*] added* *conceiv'd*] *v* altered; *d* altered* from *e* *orer*] [1]*r* blotted; [2]*r* altered *men.*] .* 634 *Vn:*] *V* blotted *warre.*] .* 635 *you.*] .* 637 *prouided;*] ; altered* from , 638 *resolues.*] .*, preceded by Hand 1 . 642 *selfe*] [2]*e* followed by otiose point 643 *agen*] *n* altered, ? from *er*, ? Hand 1 646 *man?*] ? added over , 647 *Thomas.*] .* 648 *[Engine . . . page]*] hatched over* *Device*] interlined above deletion 649 *honor'd*] *d* ascender blotted *Captaine.*] .*

you come to visit your Mistres my Cosen; as if by instinct, she
Enter Ladie and Sister, & Dorothy
had knowledge of your approach, she is come to meet you.
shall I neuer gett oportunitie with that shee waiter, If I gett her
with Child, my man Thomas shall marry her.

Enter Thomas.

Tho: Sir the Captaine is new alighted?

Vn: gett a botle of Sack vp to my Chamber presently. Ext

La: You are a gentleman of your word, [FOL. 20a]

Sis: and such a gentleman is to be trusted Madam.

De: he is an Infidell that will breake his word with a Ladie,

Sis. I suspect servant you haue many Mistresses,

De: Not I, by this white hand, I must acknowledge
there are some Ladies in the Court, in whose eyes and opinion
I am fauour'd, I cannot obscure my selfe from their
obseruation, but my heart with contempt[ment] of all
other endeerement, is onely deuoted to your
Seruice.

Sis: Is't not a charge to dresse your selfe with such variety
of Ribbands euery day?

De: Is that your scruple?
tis the Mode to expresse our fancie, vpon euery occasion, to shew
the turne, and present state of o^{r} hope, or feares, in our Affection.
your colours to an vnderstanding Lover
carry the interpretation of the hart, as plainely, as wee
express our meaning one to another in Characters.
shall
shall I decipher my Colours to you now, here [FOL. 20b]
is Azure and Peach, Azure is constant, and peach is loue,
which signifies my constant Affection.

Sis. this is very pretty,

De. Oh, it saues the trouble of writing, where the Mistres and
Servant are learned in this amorous blazon, yesterday I wore folinort
grisdelin and Isabella, folimort is withered, grisdelin is absent,
and Isabella is beauty, which put together, express I did wither or

651 *Cosen*] otiose *m* written above *n* 652 , &] added* 653 *you.*] .* 654 *waiter,*] , preceding . 658 *presently.*] .*, preceded by Hand 1 . 665 *selfe*] [1]*e* altered from *l* 666 *contempt[ment]*] [1]*m* altered* from *n*; *pt* added*; deletion hatched over* 668 *Seruice.*] .* 670 *day?*] ?* 673 *Affection.*] .* 675 *plainely,*] , marked twice 676 *Characters.*] .* 678 *loue,*] ,* 679 *Affection.*] .* 680 *very*] *r* stem partly erased *pretty*] *p* altered from *v* 683 *folimort*] *i* added*

languish for your absent beautie.
Sis. but is there any reason for theis distinctions?
De: yes lady for example yor ffollimort is a withred leafe w^{c}h doth moralise \a decay/
your yellow is ioy because –
la: why yellow sir is Iealous.
De. No, [if] yor Lemon colour, a pale kind of yellow is Iealous, yor yellow is [p*re*sent] \perfect/ ioy
yor white is Death, your milke white iñocence, yor black mourning,
your orange spitefull. –
your flesh colour lasciuious, yor maides blush enuied, yor red is
defiance, yor gold is auaritious, yor straw plenty, yor greene hope
your sea greene inconstant, yor violet religious, your
willowe forsaken. /
Sis. we may then comitt a solecisme, and be strangely interpreted by such [Fol. 21a]
curious expounders, in ye rash election, and wearing of o^{r} colo^{rs} I p*er*ceaue
La: tis pitty, but there should be some bookes for our instruction in this art.
De. yor Hierogliphick was the Egiptian wisdome, your Hebrew
was the [⟨.⟩] Cabala, your Roman had your Simball, or impresse,
but they [w]are now obsolete, your embleme trite and
conspicuous, your invention of Character
and Alphabeticall key tedious and not \delightfull,/ your motto or
rebus too open \and/ demonstrative, but the
Science, and curiosity of yor Colours in Ribbands, is not only instructive,
but an ornament, and the nearest Comentator of loue, for
as loue is entertain'd first by the eye, or to
speake more plaine, \as/ the obiect affected \is/ tooke in first by these
opticks, which receiue the species of y^{e} thing colord & beautifide,
So, it is answerable to nature, that in the progresse of our
passion, we should distinguish by our eye, the change or
constancy of our affections in apt, and [sufficient] \significant/ colours.
Sis. You haue tooke paines to study this learn'd heraldry,
De. it is the onley gentile knowledge or philosphie in the world, [Fol. 21b]
I will vndertake to open any man, or womans hart ⟨.⟩
La: heauen forbid!
De. tell the most secret imaginations, and designes, conclude euery
passion and scruple, if they be carefull to obserue ye artificiall

685 *beautie.*] .* 687 *a decay*] interlined above caret 690 *[present]*] deleted* *perfect*] interlined above deletion*, Hand 2; *p* altered* 691 *iñocence*] *in* altered* from *m*: tylde altered*: ^{1}c altered* *black*] altered*, ? from *blush* *mourning*] *i* dotted*, preceding Hand 1 dot 695 *religious*] ^{2}i dotted* 697 *be*] *e* altered 699 *art.*] .* 700 *Hierogliphick*] ^{1}i altered*, ? from *e* 701 *[⟨.⟩]*] erased *Cabala*] *C* altered from *l*; ^{2}a altered from *u* *Simball*] *a* altered from *o* *impresse*] *i* dotted*, preceding Hand 1 dot 702 *[w]are*] *a* altered from *e* *obsolete*] ^{1}e altered from *i* 703 *Character*] followed by two line-fillers 704 *delightfull,*] interlined above caret*, Hand 2 705 *and*] interlined above caret*, Hand 2 *the*] followed by a line-filler and further mark 709 *as*] interlined*, Hand 2 *is*] interlined above caret*, Hand 2 711 *So,*] ,* 713 *apt,*] ,* *[sufficient]*] hatched over* *significant*] interlined above deletion*, Hand 2 *colours.*] .* 716 *hart* ⟨.⟩] ⟨.⟩* 719 *carefull*] *c* altered from *a*

method of their colours.
Sis. why this may be a way of fortune telling too.
De. you say right Lady: Phisiognomy and chiromancy are but trifles,
Nay yor geomancie meere coniecturall, the erection of your
schemes, cirmcumstantiall and fallible, but yor quaint Alamode
weare of your fancie, more then astrologicall,
La: tis a kind of Divinitie.
De. you say very true Madam, and comes neere to propheticall, if
the minds of Ladies and gentlemen, were eleuated to the
iust and sublime consideration.
Sis. what paines he takes to be ridiculous?
Do: this gentleman has a notable fancie, and talkes poetically.
Sis. yes yes, he can write verses.
Do: well, I haue read Authors in my dayes, and knew y^{e} length of y^{e}. poets [FOL. 22a]
in my tyme too, which was an hexameter, and which a pentameter,
but the wits are not as they haue been, right and straite.
Sis. why Dority?
Do. why because wind is the cause of [theis] \many/ things, now if the wind bee
not in the right corner, tis the ill wind our prouerbe speakes of,
that blowes nobodie good, for when vapors and wind flie into the
head, it cannot be in two places at one[s] \time/, and that's y^{e} reason yor men
of most wit doe seldome loue a woman, but here comes my Master
and Sir Francis. /

Enter Sir Richard and S^{r}. Francis, and M^{r}. Courtwell.

Ri: this is a double hono^{r} to vs sir Francis, I shall want language,
but not a friendly hart to entertaine you, and yor Noble kinsman,
what my Exquisite Caualier Device? tis to no purpose
I see, to remoue into the Countrey to saue charges, and be quiet,
the whole City will come hither if I stay. I haue no stomack \to/ my Kn^{t}.
Fra. I hope madam you will be no enemy to my kinsman.
Ri: Sister I present this gentleman, obserue and cherish him, [FOL. 22b]
he has been i'th Vniuersitie
Sis. Any degree Sir?
Co: onely Bachelour forsooth.
Ri: If he wiñe you to marriage Lady quicksiluer –.

721 *too.*] .* 722 *Lady.*] .*, followed by blot 726 *Divinitie.*] .* 731 *fancie,*] ,* *poetically.*] .*
732 ^{2}*yes*] *y* descender smudged
lines 733–42 bracketed 734 *hexameter,*] ,* *pentameter,*] ,* 735 *straite.*] .* 736 *Dority?*] ?*
737 *[theis]*] hatched over* *many*] interlined above deletion*, Hand 2 738 *in*] *i* dotted* *corner,*] ,* *of,*] ,*
739 *good,*] ,* 740 *one[s]*] *e* altered* from *c*; *s* deleted* *time*] interlined above deletion*, Hand 2 *reason*] *e* cross-bar retraced* 742 *Francis.*] .* 743 *Courtwell.*] .* 746 *Device?*] ?* 748 *to*] interlined above caret*, Hand 2
Kn.^{t}] blotted 752 *Sir?*] ?* 753 *forsooth.*] .* 754 *marriage*] *i* dotted*; ^{2}*a* interlined above caret*, Hand 2
quicksiluer-] -*

Sis. he wilbe Master of his Art.
Ri: My vote is for him –
De: I like not the induction of this riuall.
Ri: he studies now the Law,
and thats the high way to preferment Sister,
Sis. Indeed it is the high way, in which some
deliuer vp their purses, he may clime
to scarlet, but that he has too good a face,
De. Sir I hope –
Ri: troth do not sir – I meane, trouble your selfe,
he is too bashfull to p^{r}vaile vpon your spirited mistres.

Enter M^{r}. Engine

En: S^{r}. Richard.
Ri: More customers? M^{r}. Engine welcome, [FOL. 23a]
your presence was vnexpected in the Countrey.
En: 'twas my ambition with some intents
to serue you Sir, please you vouchsafe your priuacie,
I bring Affaires are worth your entertainement,
I haue rid hard.
Cou: what Cauallier's this Vncle?
Sr Fra: he is the inventer of new proiects cosen,
they say, and Patents, one that liues like a Moth
vpon the Comon wealth.
Co: he lookes like one
Ri: you will excuse me gentlemen; make much of S^{r}. Francis Madam.

Ext.

Fra: weele leaue my Nephew and your sister Madam,
and take a turne i'th garden.
Sis. You may be confident
De: I doe not like the fancie in his hat,
that gules is warre, and will be ominous. Ext
Sis. the gentleman's turnd statue, blesse me, how [FOL. 23b]
he staires vpon me, and takes roote I thinke,
it moues. and now to earth is fixt agen,
Oh now it walkes, and sadly marches this way,

755 *Art.*] .* 756 *him-*] -* 757 *like*] *i* dotted* *riuall.*] .* 763 *De.*] *D* blotted 765 *mistres.*] .*
766 *M^{r}.*] ^{r} followed by raised point 768 *Engine*] *e* added*, ? Hand 2 769 *in*] *i* dotted*, preceding Hand 1 dot
Countrey.] 70 ambition] otiose ' above *m* 774 *Vncle?*] ?* 779 *gentlemen;*] ; altered* from , *Madam.*] .*
782 *garden.*] .* 785 *ominous.*] .*
lines 786–852 bracketed 788 *agen,*] ,*

is't not a ghost? heele fright me, oh sweet sir,
speake if you can, and say who murderd you?
it points at me, my eyes, vngentle eyes,
to kill so at first sight, Ile haue my lookes
arraighned for't, and small Cupid shall be iudg,
who for your sake will make me blind as he is.
Co: Ladie –
Sis: the man's aliue agen, and has
a tongue, discretion guide it, he but sent
his soule forth of an arrand, tis returnd,
Now wee shall haue some sentences
Co: Such are the strange varieties in loue,
such heates, such desperate coldes –
Sis. No more winter and you loue me, vnlesse you can comand
the Colepits, we haue had a hard tyme on't already for [want]
want of fewell. /
Co: I'me all turnd eares, and lady long to heare you, [Fol. 24a]
but pressing to you, doubt I am too neare you,
then I would speake but cannot, nought affordes
expression, th' Alphabet's too poore for wordes,
he that knowes Loue, knowes well, that euery hower,
Loue's glad, loue's sad, loue's sweet, –
Sis. and some tymes sower.
theis wordes would goe well to a tune, pray letts heare
you sing, I doe not thinke but you can make me
a ioynture of fower nobles a yeare in Balletts,
in lamentable balletts, for your wit
I thinke lies tragicall, did not you make
the Ladies Downefall?
you expresse a passion rarely, but pray leaue
your couplets, and say something in blanck verse
before you goe,
Co: before I goe? breath not that killing language,
there is no sunne but in your eyes, and when
I

790 *is't*] '* *ghost?*] ?* 791 *you?*] ?* 795 *is.*] .* 796 *Ladie –*] –* 798 *tongue*] mark above *u* 800 *sentences*] ^{2}*s* added* 802 *coldes –*] –* 804 *[want]*] deleted* 805 *want*] added* 809 *expression,*] ,* *Alphabet's*] *p* altered from *i* 810 *hower,*] ,* 811 *loue's sweet, –*] *u* altered from *n*; –* 812 *sower.*] .* 817 *tragicall,*] . altered* from , 822 *language,*] ,*

I once take leaue \of/ those [celestiall] celestiall beames [Fol. 24b]
I meet with darkenes in my habitation,
where stretch'd on sable ground, I downe shall lay
my mournefull body, and with folded Armes
heare sadder noats [then] \vppon/ the Irish harpe,
[and while my footman plaies, sigh out my part]
and drop diuision with my brinish teares
Sis. this must be lamentable musick sure.
Co. but I haue found an Art to cure this wound,
for I with fancies pencill, will so draw
your picture in the table of my hart,
your absence shall but like darke shadowes stand
to sett you of, and see you lady better,
then Loue will lett me, when I looke vpon you
Sis. Could this be true, and meant sweet Sir to me,
I should be kinder then the gentlest spring,
that warmes the world and makes fierce beasts so tame,
and trees to swell themselues to cheerefull greene,
more iocound, then the proudest quire of birds
what
what e're they be, that in the woods so wide, [Fol. 25a]
doe sing their merry catches, sure he does
but counterfeit
Co. Oh now I see that Loue
is sweet as flowers, in their fragrant birth,
gentle as silke, and kind as Cloudes to Earth.
Sis. One rime more and you vndoe my loue for euer, out vpon't
Pedlars French is a Christian language to this, I had
rather you should put me a Case out of Litleton,
they say you are a pretty Lawyer.
Co: Tenant per la Curtesie d'engleterre est, lon home
prent feme seisie in fee simple, ou e^{t} fee taile
generall, ou seisie come heire dela taile speciall
et ad issue per mesme la fame, male ou female
oies ou uife, soit lissue apres mort, ou envie

824 *of*] interlined*, probably Hand 3 *[celestiall]*] hatched over* 825 *habitation,*] ,* 827 *with*] *h* lower portion faded *Armes*] *s* altered* from ,, probably Hand 3 828 *[then]*] single-stroke deletion, probably Hand 3 *vppon*] interlined above deletion with caret*, Hand 3 829 *[and . . . part]*] single-stroke deletion*, probably Hand 3; line above *and* and below *out my part* 831 *lamentable*] [1]*l* altered from first stroke of *r* *sure.*] .* 832 *wound,*] ,* 833 *pencill,*] ,* 834 *hart,*] ,* 837 *me,*] ,* 840 *world*] *d* blotted 842 *iocound*] *i* dotted*; *ou* altered* 843 *e're*] double apostrophe 846 *Co.*] marginal blot before *C* 853 *d'engleterre*] '* 854 *seisie*] [1]*i* and [2]*i* dotted* *in*] *i* dotted*, preceded by Hand 1 dot *simple*] *i* dotted*, preceded by Hand 1 dot 856 *mesme*] first minim of [2]*m* dotted* 857 *uife*] *u* first minim dotted* [2]*ou*] altered

Si la feme de aie, la baron tiendra la [terr]
terre durant sa vie, per la ley dengleterre –
Sis. Nay here's enough a Conscience, what a Noise this confusion [FOL. 25b]
of languages make, tis almost as good as a beare baiting,
harke you Sir, you are neuer like to recouer me by law
Co: you are not the first sweet Ladie, ha's been ouerthrowne
at Com̄on lawe.
Sis. Not by tenn thousand Sir, confest, but I haue no mind to
come to issue with a Lawyer, when he should consider
my Cause at home, hee'le be at Westminster teaching
men the Statuts, No, no, I wo'not marry a Iudge
Co: why lady
Sis they are casuall things, and men that hold such strange opinons
Co. Lady you may be misinform'd, Astrea
hath not quite left the Earth, and the abuses
of some which shame the calling, are but like
Patches of beauty, on the face of lawe,
to sett the Natiue whitenes of,
Sis: farewell Sir, [FOL. 26a]
you are in loue with a barrd gowne, not beauty.
If you will be my learned Connsell, leaue it.
this yong thing is a foole, or a fine fellow.
Exit
Co. She kicks and flings out like a Colt vnwayed,
her witt's a better portion then her money,
I would not loue her yet, and I could helpe it,
My Vncle and his Mistres? I'le not hinder em.
Ex:

Enter Sir Francis and Ladie

La: It is no hono^{r} Sir, if arm'd with so
much eloquence you ouercome a woman,
I blush to say I loue you now too much,
I wish you would release, what your sweet charmes
won from my tongue, I shall repent my promise,
S^{r}. Fr: Make me not miserable after so much blessing,

858 *[terr]*] single-stroke deletion 866 *he*] *h* altered 870 *opinons*] *n* dotted 871 *misinform'd*] ^{2}*m* interlined above caret*
lines 873 (*are but like*), 874–5 bracketed 877 *beauty.*] .* added to Hand 1 , 878 *it.*] .* 884 *Mistres?*] ?* *em.*] .* above faint Hand 1 . 889 *much,*] ,* above Hand 1 , 890 *charmes*] *r* altered* 891 *repent*] ^{1}*e* upper loop retraced* *promise,*] ,* 892 *blessing,*] ,*

why Madam 'tis on honourable tearmes,
Since
Since not vpon the first attempt, but after [Fol. 26b]
a tedious seige to your faire loue, you giue vp
what shall enrich vs both, it were a sinne
to feare you can retract, what both our lipps
haue seal'd, and loose a happines so neare,
and so secure, your husband holds his pleasure
of early hunting constant, and when he
pursues the tymerous hare tomorrow morne,
Cupid will waite, to bring me to Elizium,
your bed, where euery kisse shall new create vs.
La: you must be wise in your excuse, to quit
his importunitie
Fra. Co: leaue that to me
I weare not worth the name of him, that seru'd you
to loose my glorious hope, for want of such
a thinne device, in your thought wish me prosper,
and
and I am fortifide against the power [Fol. 27a]
of fate to seperate vs, and when thou art
within the amorous circle of my armes,
we will make lawes to loue, teach tyme new motion,
or chaine him with the cordage of his haire,
like a tame thing, to walke; and watch our pillow,
and be our pleasures Centinell. /
La. I see.
My husband, tis not safe, he should obserue vs,
be wise and constant. /
S^{r}. Fra: All that's sweet attend thee. – Exit Lady
So I am sailing now to my owne Indies,
and see the happie Coast too, how my wings
doe spread to catch the wind, which comes to court 'em,
and the green Sea, Enamour'd on my barke,
doth leap to see how Cupid sitts at helme,

893 *why*] blot above *w* *tearmes,*] ,* 898 *haue*] *h* altered from *h* 900 *constant,*] *s* added*; , marked twice 902 *waite,*] ,* *Elizium*] ^{2}*i* dotted* 903 *vs.*] *v* altered from *o*; .* 906 *Co:*] *:* altered* from . 907 *him,*] ,* 909 *in*] *i* dotted*, preceded by Hand 1 dot *prosper,*] ,* 910 *fortifide*] ^{1}*i* dotted*, preceding Hand 1 dot; ^{2}*i* dotted*, above Hand 1 dot *against*] *i* dotted* 913 *motion,*] ,* 914 *haire,*] ,* 915 *pillow*] *i* dotted*, preceded by Hand 1 dot 918 *should*] *ld* base partly erased 919 *constant.*] .* above Hand 1 . 920 *thee.*] .* 923 *'em,*] ,* 924 *barke,*] ,* 925 *helme,*] ,*

and steeres my soule to his new world.

Enter Sir Richard, and Engine [FOL. 27b]

S[r]. Ri: A Monopolie say you
for Perriwiggs?

En. Is't not a rare designe, and by such art
and reasons I can name, most beneficiall
to the Com̃on wealth, preuenting the diseases,
which some vnwholsome haire breeds in mens heads,
it will be worth our agitation Sir.
and you after the rate of euery thousand
per Annū milk'd out of the comon Purse,
into your owne, may easily defaulke
to me a hundred for my first proiection.
Did I not loue you Sir, I could make choice
of other able men, that would be glad
to multiplie their money.

\S[r]/ Ri. Sir I thanke you,
but haue no mind to thriue vpon abuse of
my Princes fauour [n]or the peoples curse
here is a gentleman S[r]. Francis Courtwell [FOL. 28a]
perhapps will vndertake it

S[r]. Fr: what Sir Richard

S[r]. Ri: A Monopolie for composeing and selling of Perriwiggs.

S[r]. Fr: Excuse me Sir I dare not deale in 'em
If I be not mistaken Sir, your name
is Engine.

En. Yes Sir

Fra: the Proiector generall,
If I may aduise you sir, you should make your Will
take some convenient Phisicke[ian] and dye tymely,
to saue your credit, and an execution –
it is thought else –

En: ah –

Fra: what aile you Sir?

En. a Megrim in my head.

926 *world.*] .*, above Hand 1 . 929 *Perriwiggs?*] ?* 931 *name,*] ,* 936 *Annū*] ^{2}*n* ɱ; *ū* added* 938 *proiection.*] .* 939 *Sir,*] ,* 940 *men,*] ,* 941 *money*] *e* cross-bar retraced* 942 *S[r]*] interlined above *Ri.* *you,*] ,* 944 *[n]or*] deletion hatched over* 948 *Perriwiggs.*] .* 950 *Sir,*] ,* 951 *Engine.*] *E* altered from *e*; .* 955 *Phisicke[ian]*] *k* altered from *c*; *e* added*; *[ian]* deleted* *tymely,*] ,* 957 *thought*] preceded by pen rest *else-*] -* 958 *ah-*] *a* altered* from *o*; -* 959 *Sir?*] *?* added* 960 *Megrim*] *e* altered *head.*] .*

S^{r}: Ri: whoes there!

Enter Thomas

Looke to Mr Engin here, he faints, and send
to your Ladie, for some Cordiall waters presently.

Tho: there is a Soueraigne Well hard by, has done [FOL. 28b]
strange Cures, please you, ile throw him into that.

Ext

Ri: though I distast his busines, I wod not
he should miscarry here, you frighted him,
but come I thinke tis supper tyme, Sir Francis,
I shall expect youle hunt with me i'th morning,
I haue a pack of Doggs sent me, will make
the Forrest ring

Fra: Ile cheerefully attend you.
I loue the sport, as earlie as you please Sir,

Ri: I wish wee had all pleasures to delight you,
but no thing wants in my true loue to serue you.

Fra: yet I must Cuckhold him, I cannot helpe it. /

Act the third

Enter Thomas with S^{r}. Richards bootes.

Tho: Sir

w^{t}hin. Ri: whoes that? Thomas

Tho: the sun̄ is vp before you, here be your bootes.

that's

Ri: that's well [FOL. 29a]

hin La: I prethe donot rise yet, it is hardly day, Sirra who bid you
call him so earlie, S^{r}. Richard wonot rise yet.

Tho: I cannot helpe it, it is none of my fault.

La: wheres Doroty?

Enter Doroty

Do: here Madam, what make you vp so soone Thomas?

Tho: O Mistres Dority, tis e'ne long of you, for betweene
sleepe and awake, yor remembrance came to me this
morning, and Thomas was vp presently.

Enter Sir Richard

961 *there!*] !* 963 *faints,*] ,* 964 *presently.*] .* 965 *by,*] ,* 966 *you,*] ,* *that.*] .* 969 *him,*] ,* 970 *Francis,*] ,* 974 *cheerefully*] ^{2}*e* altered *you.*] .*, preceded by Hand 1 . 975 *Sir,*] ,* 976 *you,*] ,* 977 *you.*] .* 979 *third*] *i* dotted* 980 *bootes.*] .* 983 *bootes.*] .* 987 *Tho:*] *:* altered* from . *fault.*] .* 988 *Doroty?*] ?* 990 *Thomas?*] ?* 991 *you,*] ,* above Hand 1 , 993 *presently.*] preceded by pen rest;.*

Ri: you must excuse me wife,
I meane to kill a brace of hares, before
you thinke tis day, Come on with my Bootes Thomas,
and Dorothy goe you to S^{r}. Francis Chamber,
tell him the Day growes old, and I am readie
our horses, and the merry hounds expect vs
la: Any excuse to leaue [vs] me. [FOL. 29b]
Ri: You may take
your ease abed still Madam, I'le not loose
one morning that invites so pleasantly,
to heare my Doggs, for a new Maidenhead, I.
'twas for these sports, and my excess of charge
I left the towne, besides the City foggs
and steame of Brickhills almost stifled me,
this Aire is pure, and all my owne,
Tho: My Ladie
Meanes, shee would haue you gett another heire
Sir for your lands, though it be against my Master
the yong Captaine, yet she speakes but reason
And now I talke o'th Captaine Sir
would you had giuen him Connsell [Sir].
Ri: to what
Tho. before he tooke this huffiñg trade vpon him, [FOL. 30a]
to haue been a man of Peace, I meane a Iustice,
Nature ha's made him fitt for both alike,
hee's now at charge to keepe a Captaine Schoolemaster,
he might haue sau'd the quateridge of his Tutor,
if I had been his Clarke, and then the incom̄e
that broken heads bring in, and new yeares guifts
from soder'd virgins, and their shee prouintialls,
whose warren must be licenc'd from our office.
Ri: Away you prating knaue,
what is he readie? Enter Dorothy
Do. Alas, hee's almost dead.
La. Ri: how Dead

995 *you*] preceded by pen rest 1001 *Any*] *y* double dotted* *[vs]*] deleted* *me.*] added* 1005 *I.*] .* 1015 *[Sir]*] single-stroke deletion*; *i* dotted* 1017 *huffiñg*] *g* tail blotted 1019 *alike,*] ,* above Hand 1 , 1020 *Schoolemaster*] *c* altered* from first stroke of *h* 1021 *Tutor*] *r* altered from *n* 1024 *prouintialls,*] ,* 1025 *office.*] .* 1026 *knaue,*] ,* 1028 *hee's*] *s* altered and blotted *dead.*] .*

Do: he ha's been troubled with a fitt o'th stone
Sir all this night, sweet gentleman, he groanes,
and sweates, and cannot –
Ri: what? [Fol. 30b]
Do: Make vrine Sir
Tho: I heard my Ladie ha's an excellent
receit to cure the Stone, she is a peece
of a rare Surgeon.
Ri: well away, and gett the horses readie sirra,
or I shall ride you, and your witt together.
Tho. Alas any foole may ride me, but I would faine
see any man ride Mistres Dorothy.
Do: how Sirra? Exit Thomas
Ri: I am sorry I must leaue such a Companion,
but more lament the Cause, I wish him health
My presence cannot serue him, Morrow wife.
I cannot loose my sport. Exit
Do: Nor shee, when you are gone,
My Lady do'es expect an other hunt's up,
la: Now I must trust thy Secresie. [Fol. 31a]
Do: you shall not doubt me Madam, and t'assure you
my faith, I haue a suit to your Ladieship,
whose grant, were there no [more] \other/ bonds vpon me,
would tye me euerlastinglie to silence.
la. what ist: but name, and I shall soone confirme thee.
Do. Our Captaine o'th traind band has been offring
to chaffer Maidenheades with me, I must
confesse, I can affect the foole, vpon
good tearmes, and could devise a plott to noose
my amorous woodcock, if you priuatlie
assist me, and dare trust me with some Iewell,
of Price, that is not knowne, which shalbe faithfully
restor'd Madam
la. I that dare trust my hono^r with thee, sha'not
suspect thy faith in any treasure else,

1031 *groanes,*] ,* 1032 *sweates,*] ,* *cannot -*] -* 1033 *what?*] ?*, preceded by .* 1037 *Surgeon.*] .* 1038 *sirra,*] *ra,* added* 1039 *together.*] .* 1041 *Dorothy.*] .* 1042 *Sirra?*] ?* 1047 *shee,*] ,* *gone,*] ,* 1048 *up,*] ,* 1049 *Secresie.*] .* 1052 *[more]*] double-stroke deletion* *other*] interlined above deletion*, Hand 2 *me*] *e* blotted 1053 *silence.*] .* 1054 *I*] altered from *a* *thee.*] .* 1057 *affect*] *a* altered 1059 *woodcock,*] ,* *if*] *i* dotted* *priuatlie*] ^{1}*i* dotted* 1064 *else,*] ,*, preceding Hand 1 .

but prethe draw the Curtaines close, while I
expect
Expect this friend, I needes must hide my blushes, [FOL. 31b]
thou maist discouer from the Gallory windowe
when they are hors'd, I tremble to consider
what I haue promis'd,
Do: tremble to meet a Ghost,
you are more fearefull then a Virgin Madam,
why this setts me alonging, but ile watch
this is the timerous world of flesh and blood.
Exit

Enter Sir Richard.

la. within – Alas what doe you meane, retire for heauens sake
My husband is not gone, I heare his voice yet,
this rashnes will vndoe my fame for euer
should he returne.
Ri: how's this? returne for heauens sake, my husband is not gone
I heard his voice, this will vndoe my fame.
it was my wife, and this is sure my bed chamber.
La: \/looking forth// I haue vndone my selfe, it is my husband.
Ri: My forehead sweats, where are you Madam? [FOL. 32a]
whome did you talke too, or take me for? ha?
asleepe alreadie, or doe I dreame? I am all wonder,
Madam –
la: Nay nay kill him, and please you sweet heart,
I cannot abide a Blackamore
Ri: how's this? – wife?
la: helpe, helpe, deare husband strangle him with one
of my Lute strings, doe, do, doe,
Ri: if shee be asleepe she was not vs'd to talke thus,
she has some hideous dreame, she spake to me to,
whome should I strangle sweet hart with a lute string?
la. the king of Morocco, I thinke.
Ri: tis so, she dreames, what strange Chimeras wee
doe fancie in our sleepe? I were best wake her

1066 *blushes,*] ,* 1069 *promis'd,*] ,* 1070 *Do:*] *D* altered from *L* *Ghost,*] ,* 1071 *Madam,*] ,* 1075 *Richard.*] . preceding , 1079 *returne.*] .* 1080 *this?*] ? altered* from . *sake,*] ,* 1082 *chamber.*] .* 1083 */looking forth/*] interlined above *La:* 1090 [1]*?*] ? lacks point 1095 *string?*] ?* 1096 *thinke.*] .* 1097 *so,*] ,* *dreames,*] ,*

Madam, Madam.
la. Oh Murder, Murder [FOL. 32b]
Ri: Sweet heart – Madam wake.
la: whoe's that?
Ri: tis I.
la: Sir Richard – oh you haue deliuered me from such a dreame
I quake to thinke vpon't.
Ri: I must confesse you frighted me at first.

Enter Dorothy

Do: My Master come back? if he had found the sick
Sir ffrancis here.
Ri: how now, art thou frighted too?
Do: frighted quoth a. oh Madam the key of the Closet quickly
I must haue some Cordiall water for Sir Francis
I feare this fitt will kill him
la. Alas good gentleman make hast
Do: his appearance would betray all.
I thus preuent it?

Exit

la. Nay sweet hart you sha'not leaue me, till I ha told [FOL. 33a]
what a cruell Dreame I had, me thought a king
of Blackamores was in loue with me, and haueing
by flattering Courtship drawne me to his bedchamber,
with my consent, or force swore to enioy mee,
I knew not by what reasons to divert
the Rauisher, but told him, that I heard
thy voice, and bid him if he lou'd his life
retire, for thou wouldst deere revenge my hono^{r},
but he pursueing me, I cry'd out Murder,
at which sad noise, me thought I saw thee enter,
but hauing nere a sword, I counselld thee
to strangle him with a Lute string, for wch cruelty
of mine, me thought he [d]threw an Arrow at me,
which, if thou had'st not wak'd me, as thou did'st,
would as I slept, with my strong feares ha killd me.

1103 *I.*] .* 1106 *first.*] .* 1108 *back?*] ?* 1109 *here.*] .*, preceded by Hand 1 , 1111 *a.*] .* 1115 *appearance*] ^{1}*e* added* *betray*] *a* altered from *y* *all.*] .* 1121 *bedchamber,*] ,* 1122 *mee,*] ,* 1123 *to*] *t* altered from *d* 1124 *Rauisher*] *i* dotted* 1125 *if*] otiose . after *f* 1126 *hono^{r},*] ,* 1127 *Murder,*] ,*, preceded by Hand 1 , 1128 *enter,*] ,* 1129 *counselld*] otiose mark above *e* 1131 *[d]threw*] *th* interlined above deletion* 1133 *slept,*] ,* *me.*] .*

Ri. This was the king of Morocco, well I'me glad, [FOL. 33b]
I came to take away thy fright.
la: But sweet, you left me with a resolution,
to hunt this morning, haue you done already?
Ri: the theeues preuented me.
My Stable has been rob'd to night, two geldings
and my roane Nagg are vanished.
la: how?
Ri: Nay doe not thou vexe.
I haue sent hue and cry's, that may oretake [th]'em,
but come, Ile leaue thee to thy glasse,
and visit Sir Francis now, shees return'd.

Enter Dorothy

how does our Noble guest?
Do. hee's pretty well, he has voided one stone since,
and now finds ease. /
Ri: tis well attend your Mistres, Exit [FOL. 34a]
la: O wench, I had almost vndone my selfe,
Come o' t'other side, reach me that Peticote,
Ile tell the Storie, as I make me ready. Ext.

Enter Device Sister.

Sis Ist possible you can talke thus, and be no trauailer.
De I haue traueld in my fancie Ladie, and with y^{e} Muses, and
do for my recreation of witt compose some wonders in verse,
Poeticall essaies, as once vpon the report of a heate
that was in Egipt.
Sis. Lets heare 'em.
De. In Countreys I haue been
Vnder the Equinoctiall, where I haue seene
The Sunne disperse such a prodigious heat,
that made our siue=like skinns to raine with sweat,
Men
Men would have giuen for an Ecclipse their liues, [FOL. 34b]
Or one whisper of Aire, yet each man striues
to throw vpp grasse, feathers, nay women too

1136 *sweet,*] ,* *resolution,*] ,* 1138 *me.*] .* 1143 *cry's*] '* 1144 *glasse,*] ,* 1145 *Francis*] otiose stroke below *s* *return'd.*] .* 1147 *guest?*] ?* 1148 *since,*] ,* 1152 *Peticote,*] ,* 1153 *ready.*] .* 1155 *trauailer.*] .* 1158 *once*] *c* altered from *e* *; *e* added* *report*] *p* bowl retraced* 1159 *Egipt.*] .* 1160 *'em.*] .*
lines 1161–1210 bracketed 1165 *liues,*] ,*

to find the wind, all falls like lead, none blew,
The Dogstarre spits new fire, till't came to passe,
\Each eye became his neighbours burning glasse./
Leane men did burne to ashes presentlie,
fatt men did wast to leane Anotomye.
young womens heat did gett themselues with child,
for none but they themselues, themselues defil'd.
Old women naturally to witches turne,
and onely rubbing one an other burne.
the beasts were bak'd, skin turnd to crust, they say
and fishes in the Riuer boild away
Birds in the aire were rosted, and not burn'd,
for as they fell downe, all the way, they turn'd.

Sis. Most excellent [FOL. 35a]

De I haue seene Larkes in that motion, at fire
with an Engine of packthread perpendicular.

Sis. what would they haue giuen for a Shewer in those Conntries?

De. Now you talke of a Shewer, you shall heare
an other coppie of Verses, that I
made, of a mighty raine, which fell once in the
Indies.

Sis. that you made? if you will venture your lungs
let me heare more impossible stories to passe
away the tyme.

De. Heauen did not weepe, but in it's swelling eye,
whole Seas of Rhume, and moist Catarrs did lie,
which so bespaul'd the lower world, Men see
Corne blasted, and the fruit of euery tree,
Aire was condens't to water, 'gainst their wish, [FOL. 35b]
And all their foule was turn'd to flying Fish
like watermen they throng'd to ply a fare,
as though[⟨.⟩], it had been nauigable Aire.
beasts lost the naturall motion of each limbe,
forgott to goe, with practiseing to [sing] swim̃e
A trout now here, you would not thinke how soone

1170] interlined* 1171 *presentlie,*] ,* 1172 *Anotomye.*] .*, preceded by Hand 1 . 1173 *child,*] ,* 1174 *defil'd.*] .* 1175 *turne,*] ,* 1176 *burne.*] .* 1178 *Riuer*] *i* dotted*; *u* bowl retraced* 1179 *burn'd,*] ,* 1180 *as*] *s* altered from *l* *way,*] ,* *turn'd.*] .* 1182 *in*] *i* dotted* 1183 *perpendicular.*] .* 1186 *Verses,*] ,* 1187 *made,*] ,* *raine,*] ,* 1191 *tyme.*] .* 1192 *did*] *i* dotted*, above Hand 1 dot *eye,*] ,* 1193 *lie,*] ,* 1194 *so*] long *s* altered from *t* *world,*] ,* 1196 *'gainst*] *a* left-hand bowl, *n*, *s* retraced* 1199 *though[⟨.⟩],*] deletion, possibly [2]*t*, blotted; , added* *Aire.*] .* 1201 *goe,*] ,* *[sing]*] single-stroke deletion, probably Hand 1

taken [ready] \and/ drest for th[e]'Empero^{r} o'the Moone.
the fixed Starrs, though to our eyes were missing,
Wee knew yett were, by their continuall hissing
Weomen were mermaides, sailing with the wind,
the greatest miracle; was fish behind.
but men were all kept chast against their wish,
and could com̃itt but the cold siñ of ffish.

Sis. and that synne would puzzle all the Ciuell Lawyers
in
in the kingdome, siñs of the flesh they are perfect [FOL. 36a]
in, they know well enough what belongs to Adultry,
and simple fornication, but you would much improue
and oblige the practise of the Court, if you could bring
this siñe of fish vnder the Com̃ission, but now
I hope the raine is ouer, we shall haue faire weather.

De. Now I can tell you lady what a strange frost was
in one part of the world. –

Sis. I shall cry out fire if you doe, I had rather haue
Some discourse to keepe me warme still.

De. Or how the whole world was troubled with the
wind Collick.

Sis. No more Earthquakes I beseech you, some frends of myne
lost a great deale of land the last terme, and for ought I
know, tis neuer like to be recouer'd, why all these verses
you haue hono.rd me to heare, were translated out of
ffrench.

De You say very right lady. [FOL. 36b]

Sis. No, no, they are out of Spanish, as I remember.

De I thinke, it be out of Spanish, indeed.

Sis. Or else, the Italian.

De. troth I know not which, very well

Sis. and yet you made 'em, some gentlemen haue the faculty
to make verses, and forgett what language was the
Originall, tis Alamode I confesse sir.

De ther's the mishiefe in Poetry, A man might haue told

1203 *taken*] *k* altered* from *n*; *n* added* *[ready]*] hatched over* *and*] interlined above deletion* *th[e]'*] deleted*; '* *Moone.*] .* 1204 *Starrs,*] ,* *missing,*] ,* 1205 *were,*] ,* 1207 *miracle;*] ;* *behind.*] .* 1209 *ffish.*] .* 1215 *siñe*] *i* dotted* 1216 *weather.*] .* 1219 *if*] *i* dotted* 1220 *still.*] possibly added, ? Hand 3 1222 *Collick.*] .* 1223 *frends*] top of *s* retraced* 1228 *lady.*] .* 1229 *remember.*] .* 1230 *indeed.*] .* 1231 *Italian.*] .* 1233 *'em,*] ,* 1235 *sir.*] .*
lines 1236–8 (*rymes*) bracketed

100. lies in prose vpon his owne name, and neuer miscaried.
but leauing these rude rymes Ladie, how do you like the
Novice that Sir Richard comended

Sis. M^{r}. Courtwell?

De. Is he not a pretty Chrisome, I could not choose but
laugh, to obserue, in what rurall deportment he
came to salute you, that should haue made his address
in theis postures. /

Sis. tis enough Sir, I apprehend what you would doe, the [Fol. 37a]
truth is, touching that thing in black, I doe not loue him.

De. I know't, tis impossible

Sis why ist impossible? the man's a pretty indifferent meaning
man, but I must haue one of a more active spiritt,
no no, the man's a Coward.

De. he lookes like one

Sis. I put him too't, he dares not fight, and he that expects my
fauour to so high a degree as marriage, must be none
of my Lord Maiors whifflers, he must be valiant
in Armes, I am not taken with a ring, or Carkanet,
as some auaritious ladies, he that presents me w^{t}h the
Sword of his riuall, is more welcome, then all the silken
soft [named] natur'd six hundreds a yeere, that will be baffeld
in their best clothes, and goe downe into the Country eu^{r}y Vaca*c*ion,
like Atturneys, to be beaten against next terme, and get damage
by it; but I forget some affaires that concerne me; I take
my
my leaue, your deserts vpon me are eminent, and many, [Fol. 37b]
and for all your noble seruices I – will promise yo^{u}, nothing
you apprehend me.

De. Oh sweet lady, tis too much.

Sis. I am so wearie I can stay no longer w'ee. Exit.

De you make me ouer happie. so. so, the matters done,
I may invite my friends, hum? well thought vpon!
I shall leaue her ioyes without any bound to entertaine \me/ if I
first beat this foolish riuall of mine, and present

1237 *miscaried.*] .* 1240 *Courtwell?*] ?* 1241 *De.*] altered from *Sis.* 1246 *is,*] ,* 1248 *impossible?*] ? altered* from , 1255 *Armes,*] ,* 1258 *[named]* single-stroke deletion *hundreds*] *s* added* *yeere,*] ,* 1261 *it;*] ; altered* from , *me;*] blot beside point of ; 1262 *many,*] ,* 1264 *me.*] .* 1265 *much.*] .*, preceded by Hand 1 . 1266 *w'ee.*] .* *Exit.*] added* 1268 *vpon!*] !* 1269 *me*] interlined above caret*

her with his sword, she assures me he dares not fight,
it shall be so, thus with one baffling and disarming him,
I shall secure my Mistresse, and gett the reputation of a
fighting Cauallier, which may saue me many a knock
hereafter, among men of strong faith, that shall heare
how much hono^{r}, I haue elsewhere taken vpon the ticket

Enter Captaine and Vnderwitt:

Cap: Stand right to your files – make euen your rankes. [Fol. 38a]
Silence.
front to the right hand.
As you were,
to the righthand about,
by the lefthand,
as you were.
rankes to the right double,
rankes as you were,
rankes to the left double,
Midlemen to the righthand, double the front, as you
were to the left double the front, middlemen to ye right entire
[or by diuision] double ye front, files to the right, to ye left, to ye right
hand countermarch, to the right, to ye left, wheele about

Cap: ran tan, enough, you must not wast your lunges
too much at once, march faire, and make a Captaine.
when these words of Com̄and, are rotten, wee
will sowe some other military seedes,
you beare a braine, and memory.

Vn: I hope so, [Fol. 38b]
and now you are chose a Captaine for your Countrey,
you must giue good example to your Soldiers,
and cherish nature after exercise,
you must drinke sack.[,] sack is a fortifier,
Come, wee'le to the tauerne.

Vn: with all my heart.

Enter Mr Courtwell

here's M^{r}. Courtwell, lett's take him with vs,

1276 *vpon*] *o* altered* from *o*
lines 1278–91 bracketed 1279 *Silence.*] .* 1290 *[or by diuision]*] single-stroke deletion *right,*] ,*
1292 *ran*] added*, Hand 3 *tan*] altered* from *So*, Hand 3 *enough*] *e* altered*, ? from *i*, Hand 3 *lunges*] *u* retraced*
1293 *Captaine.*] .* 1296 *braine,*] ,* *memory.*] .* 1299 *your*] *ou* blotted 1301 *sack.*] .* 1305 *vs,*] ,*

Cap: My Costiue Countreyman, hee's an An[⟨.⟩]abaptist,
he wonot drinke, and yet he kist the Cupp of
last night me thought when \his/ Mistres – dranke to him.
wee'le try, how ist my man of mortall breeding?
Cou: My man of warre treboun, your seruant, Captaine.
Cap: why this was spoke like one of vs, canst doo't
agen, thy voice is more authentick, soundes
as I haue heard a Caualliers in tauerne,
or like the merry master of the Dragon,
small Neptune, that controlls the rich Canaries, [Fol. 39a]
when he Comaunds the Tritons of his cellar,
skud, and bring wine you varlotts, with a flauor,
for my Nobilitie. wee were conspiring
to goe to th' tauerne.
Cou: Ile make one gentlemen to wash away some melancholy,
Cap: Spoke boldlie like an Argona[n]ute.
Cou: I am not now in London,
vpon a hall day marching with the puisnes,
twenty on's in a teame, to westminster,
in our torne gownes, embroiderd with strand dirt,
to heare the Law.
Cap: is not thy father dead, thou talkst so well?
how I was cosend in thee? come away.

Enter Thomas.

Vn: here's my man Thomas.
Cap: Now the Newes Sir Tristram?
Tho: oh the gentleman is mad, [Fol. 39b]
Oēs what gentleman?
Tho: why M^r^. Engine, that did faint last night,
Vn with feare of being hang'd for his proiections,
Cou: My vncle told me of him,
Cap: let him to bedlam then, what makes he here?
Cleane straw and a good whip are held restoritiues.
Tho: he walkes, and talkes the madliest, twenty midwiues
are nothing to him, he drownes all their noise,

1306 *Costiue*] altered* from *Cosen* *An[⟨.⟩]abaptist*] ⟨.⟩ ? *n* 1308 *his*] interlined* *him.*] .* 1309 *try,*] , preceding Hand 1 , *breeding?*] ? point added* 1310 *treboun*] *n* altered* from *s* *Captaine.*] .* 1312 *agen,*] ,* 1313 *tauerne,*] ,* 1314 *Dragon,*] ,* 1315 *Neptune,*] ,* 1318 *Nobilitie.*] .* *conspiring*] [1]*i* dotted*, preceded by Hand 1 dot 1319 *tauerne.*] .* 1320 *melancholy,*] ,* 1321 *Argona[n]ute.*] *u* interlined above deletion*; .* 1322 *London,*] ,* 1323 *puisnes,*] ,* 1324 *westminster,*] ,* 1325 *dirt,*] ,* 1327 *well?*] ?* 1328 *thee?*] ? added* after , *away.*] .* 1330 *Thomas.*] .* 1331 *Newes*] blots following *s* *Tristram?*] ?* 1332 *mad,*] ,* 1333 *gentleman?*] ?* 1337 *here?*] ?* 1338 *restoritiues.*] .*

his tongue is twenty ring of Bells, and yett,
he seemes so merry.

Enter Engine

En. Saue you gentlemen, gallants, Caualliers, how farre
trauell you, me thinkes you \are/ very finely accomodated,
are you a Doctor Sir?
Cap: No, but I can tell you, how to purge and please you
En: you say very well, troth gentlemen you must pardon [me]
me
me cry you mercy your name is Captaine Vnderwit, [FOL. 40a]
Vn: yes Sir, but my mother came of the ouer muches
by the Peake, she broke my fathers hart, and
Sr Richard buried her, thinges must be as please
the Starres.
En. what thinke you of the blazeing starre in Germany, according to \ptolomy/
tis very strange, do'es the race hold at Newmarket for the
Cup? when is the Cocking gentlemen? there are a parcell
of rare Iewells to be sold now, and a man had money,
I doe meane to build a very fine house next summer,
and fish pondes, what, did you heare of the new play?
I am afraid the witts are broke, there be men will
make affidauit, that haue not heard a good iest since
Tarleton dyed, Pray may I craue your name Sir.
Cou: My name is Courtwell Sir.
En: in your eare, I haue a cast of the best Marlins in England,
but I am resolu'd to goe no more by water, but in my
Coach, did you euer see the great Ship?
Cap: I haue been one of twenty, that haue dind in her lanterne. [FOL. 40b]
En: it may be so, she is a good sailer, but ile \tell/ you one thing, I
meane to haue the best pack of hounds in Europe, S^{r}. Richard
loues the sport well, and then if I can but find out
the reason of the loadstone, I were happie, and would
write Non vltra.
Cap: the Philosophers stone were better in my opinion,
haue you no proiect to gett that?

lines 1344–1436 bracketed 1345 *are*] interlined above caret* 1348 *[me]*] double-stroke deletion 1354 *ptolomy*] interlined above caret 1356 *gentlemen?*] ? added* over , 1359 *play?*] ?* 1362 *Sir.*] .* 1363 *Sir.*] .* 1364 *Marlins*] *a* altered from *e* 1366 *Ship?*] ? point added*, preceded by Hand 1 point 1367 *twenty,*] ,* *lanterne.*] .* 1368 *is*] *i* dotted* *sailer*] *i* dotted*, preceded by Hand 1 dot *ile*] *i* dotted*, preceded by Hand 1 dot *tell*] interlined above caret*

Cou: that has startled him; I doubt this fellow does but
Counterfeit.
Vn: what thinke you of the Dromedary, that was to be seene i'th
back side of the Bell?
En: I haue seene a stranger beast,
Cap: So haue I. I haue seene you, before now sir.
En. why then ile tell you, the strangest beast that euer I saw
was an Ostridge, that eate vp the Iron mynes, but now you
talke of birds, I saw an Elephant beat a Taylor in the
fenceing schoole, at his owne weapon.
Tho: the Spanish Needle? [FOL. 41a]
En. he did out eat him in bread, and that was miraculous,
I haue seene a Catamountaine once, but all was nothing
to the [lady] \wench/ that turnd round, and thred needles
Cou. troth Sir I thinke you haue turnd round too, and are not setled yet,
En: Now you talke of setling, I knew a gentleman, that was
borne to a good fortune, sold all his land, went to sea in a
hollander, was taken by the Dunkerke, \at/ seauen yeares end
stole away in an English botome \after/ that, saw both the Indies,
for all this was taken by a turks man of warre,
put into the Gallies, and for ought I heare by credible report
is not setled yet.
Tho: Sure he is a great scholler, a man cannot vnderstand him,
Vn: his braines are out of tune.
En: Now you talke of Musick, there's no man in the world
loues musick, better then I, ile giue you the reason[s],
I haue been deafe almost this halfe yeare, and it came
with a cold sitting vp a Primero.
Cou: Now you talke of the cold it puts me in mind of the [FOL. 41b]
new device of fire, for brewing, and bakeing, had you no
hand in that proiect?
Cap: againe hee's startled, come he shall to tauerne with vs,
and confess all, if he do not strip his soule starkenaked
to vs, say I am no fortune teller?
[Vn. what think you of a Cup of medeira wine]?

1375 *him;*] *;* altered* from , 1378 *side*] *i* dotted*, preceding Hand 1 dot 1380, 1381 *you,*] ,* 1382 *Ostridge,*] ,* 1383 *birds,*] ,* 1384 *schoole,*] ,* 1385 *Needle?*] *?** 1388 *[lady]*] hatched over* *wench*] interlined above deletion* 1390 *gentleman,*] ,* 1392 *at*] interlined* *end*] *e* altered* from *a* 1393 *away*] *w* final minim retraced* *after*] interlined above caret* *that,*] ,* 1395 *Gallies,*] ,* *credible*] *c* altered from *r* 1396 *is*] *i* dotted* *not*] *n* altered from *s* *yet.*] .*, preceded by Hand 1 . 1397 *Sure*] *u* retraced *him,*] ,* 1398 *tune.*] .* 1399 *Musick,*] ,* over Hand 1 , 1400 *musick,*] ,* *reason[s]*] deleted* 1401 *been*] *ee* altered from *e* 1402 *Primero.*] .* 1403 *mind*] *i* dotted* 1404 *fire,*] ,* *brewing,*] ,* 1405 *proiect?*] *?* point added* 1408 *vs,*] ,* 1409–10 *[Vn . . . all]*] hatched over*

[Cap: that will spoile all], please you to hono^{r} our society,
we are going to indulge at the tauerne hard by.
En: you shall comand me Sir, oh the Neats tongues, and
partargoes, that I haue eaten at Stillyard, but of all
things in the world, I do not loue a black Catt, next a
brewers Cart, there's nothing will stay a man so much in the
night as a Constable, one word before you \go/ and I beseech
you giue me your opinion cleerely, was not y^{e} Morocco
Ambasado^{r} a very fine gentleman, for a Pagan?
Cap. yes surely, and the lead mines in Darbisheire hold still,
marry for the Allom-businesses – but come will you walke S^{r}.
En: I do vse to goe a foote sometymes, but when I ride, [FOL. 42a]
and then I must confesse, there is no striving
with the streame, you were in London lately
they say the people are more affected to beare baiting
then in former tyme.
Cap: there are some a late are drawne like beares to ye stake, but for
your owne part, the gout and the grand pox are all one
to you, what price beare meat in the Shambles?
En: flesh [w]rises and falls as it vs'd to doe sir.
but a Countrey life is the best when all's done. are
wee all of one Religion? what thinke you of a bridg
from Lion key to Flaunders? you may guess I talke at
randam gentlemen, but you must not interpret all foo=
lish discourse a distemper of the braine, Lords would
take it for a Scandalum Magnatum, and yor Ladies would
bee angry too.

Enter S^{r}. Francis and Lady.

now you talke of Ladies
Cap: by no meanes M^{r}. Engin, that gentleman loues you not, [FOL. 42b]
come, ile bring vp the rere, where's Thomas?
Tho. Ile follow Sir, I would giue my fower marke a yeare,
that I could talke like that mad gentleman, hee's here,
and there and euery where, how will his tongue run, when
his Coggs are oild, the'ile drench him. Exit

1411 *indulge*] *i* dotted*, preceding Hand 1 dot *by.*] .* 1414 *world,*] ,* 1415 *Cart,*] ,*, preceding Hand 1 , 1416 *go*] interlined above caret* 1417 *cleerely,*] ,* 1418 *for*] *o* retraced* *Pagan?*] ?* 1419 *still*] ²*l* blotted 1420 *will*] *i* altered from *e* 1425 *tyme.*] .* 1429 *[w]rises*] deleted*; *r* retraced*; *i* dotted*; ¹*s* altered* *sir.*] .* 1430 *done.*] .* 1431 *Religion?*] ?*, above Hand 1 , 1432 *Flaunders?*] ?*, above Hand 1 , 1435 *Scandalum*] ²*a* altered* from *u*

lines 1437–8 bracketed 1439 *Engin,*] ,* *not,*] ,* 1440 *come,*] ,* *rere,*] ,* above Hand 1 , 1441 *Sir,*] ,* *yeare,*] ,* 1442 *here,*] ,* 1444 *him.*] .*

\S^{r}/ Fra: Although I mist a happines, I applaud
your nimble wit, that secur'd both our hono^{rs},
you haue an excellent Instrument too, ô yor gentlewoman
la: Oh she deliuer'd so to th' life, how you
were troubled with the Stone, at first, I did
beleeu't my selfe, and thinke of the sad consequence.
but tyme is pretious now, although our starres
haue not been yet propitious to our meeting,
ile try my art tonight, to make 'em shine
with happie influence [of] \on/ our Loues
Fra: Most excellent Madam how?
la. Ile not engage [Fol. 43a]
your visit to my chamber, since the first
prou'd so vnfortunate, but come to yours,
Fra this night? wonot your husband be at home?
la. Yes.
Fra: you enioy but one bed.
la: without witchcraft sir,
I haue a stratage͞me to delude my husband,
and all his Iealous, waking eyes, a plott,
that cannot faile, if you dare but expect me,
Fra: I grow im̄ortall with my hopes, and fancie
more then the worlds most pretious Empire, in
our first embrace, I should \runne/ back in to
an Infant once agen, and by degrees,
and tyme grow vp, to meet so vast a happines.
Ages in expectation spent, were poore
and easy sufferings, weigh'd against this triumph.
Me thinkes I am not man, but something of [Fol. 43b]
A more exalted essence, humane nature
hath not capacity, to understand,
and owne theis spatious blessings.
La: No more rapture,
but with the confidence of a Louer, spread
your equall thoughts, \and/ in your heart, and armes

1445 *S^{r}*] interlined above *Fra:* *mist*] *i* dotted*, preceding Hand 1 dot 1449 *first,*] ,* 1450 *consequence.*] .* 1452 *meeting,*] ,* 1454 *[of]*] single-stroke deletion *on*] interlined, probably Hand 1 1455 *how?*] *?* point added* 1456 *engage*] followed by pen rest 1458 *yours,*] ,* 1459 *home?*] *?** 1460 *Yes.*] .* 1461 *Fra:*] *F* lacks cross-bar *bed.*] .* 1462 *sir,*] ,* 1464 *Iealous,*] ,* 1468 *embrace,*] ,* *runne*] interlined above caret 1469 *an*] otiose point after *n* 1470 *happines.*] .* 1472 *triumph.*] *h* altered* from *l*; .* 1476 *blessings.*] *i* dotted*; .* 1477 *La:*] *La* added , Hand 1 *rapture,*] ,* 1479 *thoughts,*] ,* *and*] interlined*, ? Hand 1 *in*] *i* dotted* *heart,*] ,*

prepare an entertainement for that guest,
that hath no life, or name, but what you give.
a kisse; and leaue our soules to thinke vpon
the [ioynes] ioyes this night attend vs.

Fra: Sullen Day
do not tire now, tis downehill all the way.

(Exeunt seuerally)

Act the fourth

A Song i'th tauerne

Enter Thomas. /

Tho: they are all drunke already, and such Confusion in their [Fol. 44a]
heads and tongues, my master kisses the next man, and
calls him Mistres Dorothy, M^{r}. Courtwell, possest [with]
with the spiritt of defiance to Cupid, is ready to beat him
for being in loue, my Proiector dead drunke in a Chaire,
and the Captaine peepeing into his mouth like a tooth drawer,
and powring downe sack, which he feeles not, but his chap'ps
shut againe like a spring lock, till he returne w^{t}h a key
to open his teeth, to poure in the next health.

Enter Courtwell

Cou: My Cloake and sword Drawer.

Tho: tis here sir.

Cou: thou art a pretty fellow here's halfe a Crowne, say I
am gone Thomas.

Tho: you are pretty well.

Enter Captaine and Vnderwitt

Vn: what shalls doe with him, this Engin burnes like Etna.

Cap: throw him into the River. [Fol. 44b]

Vn. hee's able to [wade] mull the Thames, well, for my owne part would
Mistresse Dorothy were here, to open her files.

Cou: Did you not name a woman?
I will haue no mention of any thing that's female,

Vn: May not a man talke of Sack?

Cap: Sack is a Soueraigne medicine

Vn: Oh very Soueraigne!

1480 *guest,*] ,* 1481 *life,*] ,* *give.*] .* 1482 *kisse;*] ; altered* from , 1483 *[ioynes]*] single-stroke deletion *vs.*] .* 1484 *Fra:*] *F* lacks cross-bar 1485 *downehill*] *e* added* *way.*] .* 1490 *their*] altered from *her* 1491 *heads*] *d* ascender retraced* 1492 *[with]*] single-stroke deletion 1493 *spiritt*] ^{2}*i* dotted*, preceding Hand 1 dot *Cupid,*] ,* 1494 *Proiector*] *i* dotted* *drunke*] *u* second minim retraced* *Chaire,*] ,* 1495 *drawer,*] ,* 1496 *sack,*] ,* 1497 *lock,*] ,* 1498 *teeth,*] ,* *health.*] .* 1499 *Enter*] added*, probably Hand 1; blot above *e* 1500 *Drawer.*] .*, preceding Hand 1 . 1501 *sir.*] .* 1503 *Thomas.*] .* 1504 *well.*] .*
lines 1505–41 bracketed 1505 *Enter*] added*, probably Hand 1 1506 *Etna.*] .* 1507 *River.*] .* 1508 *[wade]*] hatched over* *mull*] interlined above deletion, ? Hand 2 1509 *Mistresse*] *i* altered from *e* *here,*] ,* *files.*] .* 1510 *Did*] *i* altered 1512 *Sack?*] ?*

Cap: Is it not, hic, et hec sack, both for he and she, stay –
is my Countryman gone?

Capt. Come my Apollo's, my Orpheuse's, or my Bacchus his Minstr⟨ [FOL. 78+a]
wch to leaue Poeticall expressions \in broader phrase/ is Tauerne ffidlers, Som⟨
of yor new Tunes my Masters, doe yo^{u}: heare?

1. Doe yo^{u} meane M^{r}. Adson's new ayre's S^{r}?

Capt. I S^{r}, but they are such phantasticall ayres, as it putts
a Poet out of his witts to rhime to them, but let mee
heare?

1. [Hee] They [singes] Play.

Capt. No I doe not like that!

1. [Hee] They [singes] \Play/ againe;

Capt. Nor that (Play againe.)– – No, no, no, neither.

[The Musique Playes.]

1. An't please yor Worship Mr Capt, our Boyes can singe
songs to these.

Capt. No, no! saueing yor presence yor Boyes haue nothing
surreuerence but Loue songs, & I hate those monstruous⟨ly⟩
to make thinges appeare better than they are, and that is
but deceptio Visus, wch after some embraceing the[y] partie⟨s⟩
see presently what it is.

ee sings & reeles
illips all the
ile wth his
ger. Then says,

* The Musique Playes.

Capt. I, I, this [this] thumping tune I like a life. a Song, a song
to it.

One Singes

Verte

This Song. [FOL. 78+b]

The Iuice of Spanish squeez'd Grapes is It,
That makes a dull Braine so full of witt,
So Lemonados cleere sparkling wine,
The grosser witts too doth much refine,
Then to bee fox'd, It is no crime,
Since thickest & dull Braines It makes sublime.

1515 *it*] *i* dotted* *she*] *s* retraced*; secretary *e* altered from Greek *e* 1516 *gone?*] *?* added* above Hand 1 , 1517] Hand 4 addition inserted here *Orpheuse's*] ^{2}*s* blotted *Minstr*⟨] *els* cut off in outer margin 1518 *in broader phrase*] interlined above caret *Som*⟨] cut off in outer margin 1524 *They*] altered* from *Hee* 1526 *They*] altered* from *Hee* *Play*] interlined above deletion 1531 *nothing*] followed by one line-filler 1532 *monstruous*⟨*ly*⟩] *ly* cut off in outer margin; base of *l* and tail of *y* visible 1534 *partie*⟨*s*⟩] *s* cut off in outer margin; base just visible lines 1543–1656 bracketed 1545 *Lemonados*] ^{1}*o* altered from *a*

The Stillyard's Reanish wine & Diuell's white
Who doth not in them sometimes take delight.
If wth Mimique Gestures you'le keep yo^{u} from sadnes
Then drinke lusty Clarett 'twill [make] \putt/ yo^{u} in Madnes.
And then to settle you, no hop[p]es in Beere
But wholesome Potts of Scotch Ale, though 'tis deere. /

Capt. But looke yo^{u} Child yo^{u} say the Diuell's white, in yor song,
You haue beene ill [Cathec] Catechiz'd, Boy, for a white
Diuell is but a Poeticall fiction, for the Diuell, God
blesse vs Child is blacke. /

Boy. No Capt, I say white wine at the Diuell. /

Capt. That's true! thats a good Boy indeed.
Vnderwitt, lend mee a Peice to giue these Harmonious me⟨n⟩
there – and now begon my Masters, wthout noise for
I will haue no more fiddle faddles for my money, [⟨S.....⟩]
[Thomas] – [(Hee singes)] No tunes of supererrogation
after the Musicall Bill is paid. /
And then begin as was intended,
come hither Thomas, [FOL. 44b]
do you thinke I am drunke?

Tho: truly Captaine I cannot tell,

Cap: you cannot tell, there's your ignorance, drink is a \vice/
I am as litle giuen to as another man, for I doe
abhorre it in my selfe, I do wonder how any reasonable
man can be drunk, therefore euery wise man take
Counsell, and example by me, and he may see very
plainely
plainely what an odious thing it is, for you must [FOL. 45a]
follow your leader, and vertue, w^{c}h is an Antient –

Tho: Vertue an Antient?

Cap: I, an Antient old gentlewoman, that is growne
very poore, and nobodie knowes where she dwells,
very hard to find her out, especially for a Capt.
you will find it very difficult for a Livetenant,
but wee will endeauour the best wee can,

1552 *[make]*] single-stroke deletion, ? Hand 3 *putt*] interlined above deletion with caret, Hand 3 1553 *hop[p]es*] *e* interlined above deletion with caret, probably Hand 3 *Beere*] ²*e* altered from *a* 1555 *Child*] *d* blotted 1561 *me⟨n⟩*] *n* cut off in outer margin; first minim just visible 1565a] Hand 4 addition ends 1566 *come . . . Thomas,*] second half of line 1516, Hand 1 1569 *vice*] interlined above caret 1580 *for*] preceded by pen rest 1581 *can,*] ,*, preceded by Hand 1 ,

you see my courses, I haue trauel'd to find her
out, and I could neuer yet see her at a baudihouse.

Vn. who is to be seene at a baudihouse? to y^{e} righthand counter-\march/

Tho: he talkes of vertue sir.

Vn: Vertue, she neuer comes there, why do you thinke she
should be there Captaine?

Ca: why, because she is an old gentlewoman, and might keepe y^{e} house.

Tho: Alas Captaine M^{ris}. Vertue is poore, and leane.

Ca: Nay, then she is not fit to be a baud, but tell me, [FOL. 45b]
did you euer see her, or if so did you euer doo't wth her?

Vn: No, but twas none of my fault, I know not what I may do in
tyme, when she vnderstands the wordes of Comand.

Tho: he do'es non meane \M^{ris}/ Dorothy, but Captaine, I would
faine know the reason, why your baudes are so fat still?

Cap: a plaine Case, they lie fallow, and get hart, then they keepe
themselues so in health, and so sol[a]uble with stewd prunes,
and then sipping of sack is a great matter to fatten 'em.
but they are as good people, as a man shall keepe company
withall, and bring vp the young gentlewomen so vertuously,
I came into one of their houses t'other day for a Carreere
and I found the baud [very] sick vpon her death bead, very
religious, and much giuen to repentance, for those poore
siñs she had comitted, when she had taken order for
her soule, she told me the yong gentlewoman I look'd for, was
in the next roome, and desiring her vpon her blessing [FOL. 46a]
to giue me content, she turnes her selfe to ye wall.
and giues vp the ghost very priuatly, because she
was loath to trouble vs.

Vn. by your relation, theis appeare to be very good people,
what if we went to visit one of these Matrons, I haue a
great mind –

Ca: Wy, now you speake like an vnderstanding soldier, and
one that may come to something in the end, Lett vs
therefore march on.

Vn: March on to Venus warres.

1582 *trauel'd*] *e* altered from *a*, probably Hand 1 1584 *baudihouse?*] *?* added* above Hand 1 , *march*] interlined above caret 1589 *poore,*] ,* *leane.*] .*, above Hand 1 . 1593 *Comand.*] .* 1594 *M^{ris}*] interlined above caret 1597 *sol[a]uble*] *u* interlined above deletion* 1598 *'em.*] .* 1599 *people,*] ,* 1600 *gentlewomen*] *g* top of bowl and tail retraced* *vertuously*] ^{1}*u* altered from *o*, ? Hand 1 1601 *came*] *e* added* 1602 *[very]*] single-stroke deletion* 1604 *order*] ^{2}*r* blotted 1607 *wall.*] .*, preceded by Hand 1 ,

Cap: for you know Thomas, that the spider, and the Bee, the
spider and the Bee, do [but] both – something but in troth
I haue forgott what tis.
Vn. tis no matter what, let vs goe –
Ca: goe, no more but goe, though I be a Captaine, if I be not
chosen in this imployment,
Tho: what then Captaine? [FOL. 46b]
Cap: why then – I cannot goe –
Tho. Very right –
but wo'not those yong gentlewomen you talk'd of giue a
man something to make a man afraid of pepper vpon
occasion?
Cap. you will be prating so long, till I breake your head,
for pretending to that, which you haue not Sirra
Tho Alas I neuer had it in my life.
Vn. what's that Captaine?
Cap. wit, I talke of wit?
Vn. who has any wit?
does my man offer to haue wit?
Cap. Nay nay take no offence at it,
for I meant none to either of you, by this sack
Drawer, giue me my oath, cannot you drinke without
wit? cannot you game without wit?
Vn: and yet by yor fauo^{r}, the gamesters are cald the [best] wits now, [FOL. 47a]
Cap. tis no wit to Cozen, confederacy, and dishonesty will
doo't without wit, ile iustifie it, do not you know the
receit of Cozenage? take an ounce of knauery
at the least, and confederacie is but so many knaues put
together, then you must take a very fine yong Codling
heire, and pound him as small as you can;
Vn. and what then Captaine?
Ca: why then you must cozen him.
Vn: but which way?
Ca: which way, why which way you will, is not cosen him enough?
thou art a pretty fellow, ile talke with thee, thy name's

1617 *Bee,*] ,* 1618 *[but]* deleted* 1620 *what,*] ,* *vs*] *v* misformed 1622 *in*] *i* dotted*, preceded by Hand 1 dot stroke deletion 1623 *Captaine?*] ?* 1626 *wo'not*] '* 1629 *head,*] ,* 1631 *life.*] .* 1640 *[best]*] single-stroke deletion 1650 *enough?*] ?*

Thomas, take heed I say still Thomas, of being drunke, for it doth
drowne the im̃ortall soule, and yo[rs] cannot swim Thomas,
can it?

Tho: Not as I know Captaine, if it scape fire, tis as much
as I looke for.

within [FOL. 47b]

Eng: – oh – oh.

Cap: what's that.

Tho: tis M[r] Engine recouerd from his dead sleepe. ex.

Vn: d'ee heare Captaine, for all this, I haue a great mind
to a wench, and a wench I must haue, if there be one
aboue ground, oh london, london, thou art full of frank
tenements, giue me London, shall we wheele about yet?

Ca: giue you London, wo'nott cheapeside serue your turne,
or the Exchange? /

Enter Thomas.

Tho: Oh gentlemen, M[r]. Engine is surely bewitch'd,

Cu: what, what's the matter, bring the witch [in] and M[r]
Engine before vs.

Tho: he does vomit the strangest things yonder,

Ca: Did not I say, murder will out?

Tho: I thinke, he has eaten and dranke nothing but
Monopolies. / and too hard to be digested, they come
all vp againe.

within Eng: – oh [FOL. 48a]

Tho: harke. I must hold his head. exit

Cap: did not I tell you something would come out

Tho: Piñs Piñs, they lay cross his throat I told
you, he was bewitch'd, heyday! Cardes and dice,
out with 'em, the Diuells a gamster, and paies the
box soundly, Now, now, now.

Vn: whats that?

Tho: tis something clammy. now. oh, tis sope!

Ca: Sope? giue a man leaue to wash his mouth.

Vn: does not the lyme burne his throat Thomas?

1660 *Engine*] *e* added* *recouerd*] *er* retraced *dead*] *de* retraced* 1661 *d'ee* (*de'e*)] [1]*e* retraced *for*] *o* retraced* 1664 *we*] *w* third minim retraced* 1665 *wo'nott*] '*; *tt* retraced* *cheapeside*] *c* altered; *p* smudged 1668 *Engine*] *e* added* *bewitch'd,*] ,* 1669 *[in]*] deletion hatched over* 1670 *Engine*] *e* added* *vs.*] .*, preceding Hand 1 . 1671 *yonder,*] ,* 1672 *murder*] *u* second minim and bowl of *d* retraced* *out?*] *?* point added* 1674 *digested,*] *i* double dotted; ,* 1677 *head.*] .* *exit*] added* 1678 *would come*] *d* and *c* retraced* 1679 *Piñs,*] ,* *cross*] [2]*s* altered 1682 *now.*] . preceded by , 1684 *now.*] .* above Hand 1 , *sope!*] *!* point added* 1685 *mouth.*] .*

Tho: Alas poore gentleman, something now agen is ready
to strangle him. out with 'em, hides, hides, it was
the hornes stuck in his gullett.
within oh –
Tho. well straind! what a foule stomack he has, open
your mouth M^{r}. Engine.
Cap: thr[oat]ow downe a PottlePot. [FOL. 48b]
Tho: I haue Sir, and it has come vp full [Sir] of Medium wine[s].
if you haue any Charity, come, and helpe to hold his
head, now agen.
within Oh, oh, oh,
Vn: this is very strange, Captaine ye man is certainely enchanted,
Tho: Master, Master, tis Shrovetuesday, and the prentices are
pulling downe Covent garden, the Brickes come as whole
out, as if he had swallowed Cherristones; hey! will you take
Tobacco in the Roll, here is a whole Shiplading of Bermudas, and one
little twopenny paper of verrinas, with a superscription
To my very loving friends o'the Custome house.
Cap: Put vp that for a relique Thomas, and open it vpon high dayes
to cleare the sore eyes of our Spanish Marchants.
Thomas – no more, but call the Drawer, an vnderstanding
Drawer, and one that writes Orthographie.
Enter Dawer.
Sirra I charge you, set a Padlock vpon that Chamber
doore
doore, there is a dangerous fellow must be brought to [FOL. 49a]
his purgation, and looke all the goods that he hath
vomitted be forthcomeing, while we discreetly goe
and enforme the Magistrates, at your perill Sirra,
at your perill, Seale vp the Doore, and do you pay
the reckoninge.
Vn: S^{r}. Richard is a Iustice, there's your money, and yet wee
need not pay, the gentleman hath left enough for the
Reckoning in the next Roome.
Dra: I ha made him fast, you are very welcome gentlemen

1687 *gentleman,*] ,* 1688 *'em,*] ,* 1689 *gullett.*] .* 1691 *open*] followed by pen rest 1692 *Engine*] *e* added* 1693 *thr[oat]ow*] *ow* interlined above deletion* 1694 *[Sir]*] deletion hatched over* *wine[s]*] *i* dotted* above Hand 1 dot; deleted *; .* 1695 *his*] *i* altered from *s* 1696 *agen.*] .*, preceded by Hand 1 . 1698 *enchanted,*] ,* 1700 *Covent*] *v* retraced * 1701 *hey!*] *!* point added* 1703 *verrinas*] *i* dotted*, preceded by Hand 1 dot 1704 *house.*] .* 1706 *Marchants.*] .* 1708 *Orthographie.*] .* 1716 *reckoninge.*] .*, preceded by Hand 1 . 1719 *Roome.*] .*, preceded by Hand 1 .

All's paid in the Percullis. Exeunt
Enter Courtwell and Sister
Sis. Ile walke no further, if you haue a secret
to impart, you need not feare this place, the trees
and hedges will not listen, what's the busines?
I hope your Phlegmatick stock of verse is spent. /
Cou: why then in prose, the worst that I can speake in, [FOL. 49b]
I doe not loue you Lady,
Sis. how? you ha not
traind me thus farr, to tell me that ?
Cou. you are
of all your sex the poorest, emptiest trifle,
and one with whome, tis most impossible
I e're should change Affection, theres nothing
to invite me toot, no, not so much, as that
wee call a seeming reason, vpon which
all loue is built, seeming I say, not It
my vnderstanding Ladie.
Sis. you thinke I am very dull, that you expound
your witt thus, but it needes no Comentator,
not by the Author, tis so very plaine.
but to despise me most of all the Sexe,
is something ouersaid. though I affect
no flattery, I hate vncivill Language,
you
you do not meane to quarrell, now you haue [FOL. 50a]
betraid me to the feild, and beat me Sir?
Co: what is there in your face more to attract mee,
then that Red Cowes complexion, why the Diuell
do you thinke, I should dote vpon your person?
that thing, when she is stroak'd, giues milke.
Sis. by that,
I vnderstand all this reuenge, because
you thinke I did neglect you. Pray sir tell me,
and tell me seriouslie, put the Case, that I
should loue you now, could not you loue agen?

lines 1723–1883 bracketed 1724 *impart*] *i* dotted*, preceding Hand 1 dot 1725 *busines?*] altered* from *busine.* , Hand 2 1738 *Ladie.*] .* 1741 *plaine.*] .* 1744 *vncivill*] ^{2}*i* altered from *e* 1749 *thinke*] *t* altered from *s* 1750 *milke.*] .* 1755 *now,*] ,* *agen?*] ?*

Co: In troth I thinke I could not.
Sis. you do but thinke.
Co: Nay ile bind it with an oath, before the parish,
and when I haue giuen my reasons too, the Clarke
shall praise me fort, and say Amen
Sis. what reasons?
Co: I shall be very loath, [Fol. 50b]
to say your eyes are twinckling Starrs agen,
your lipps twin Cherries, and out blush the Rubie,
your azure Veines vye beauty with the Saphire,
Or that your swelling breasts are hills of Ivory,
pillowes for Ioue to rest his amorous head,
when my owne Conscience tells me, that Bunhill
is worth a hundred on 'em, and but Higate
compar'd with 'em is Paradice, I thanke you,
Ile not be vext and squeez'd about a rime,
or in a verse that's blanke, as I must be
whine loue [to] \vnto/ a [Beggars] tune
Sis. this all your feare?
No. No, I doe feare to loose my tyme, my businesse,
and my witts too, iolting them all away
to waite on you in prouder Coaches.
Sis. Is this all.
Co: to spend my selfe to nothing, and be laugh'd at [Fol. 51a]
by all the world, when I shall come at last
to this reward for all my seruices,
to bee your lay Court Chaplaine, and say grauely
a hastie grace before your windowes breakfast.
Sis but how
came you thus cur'd, you were a passionate,
(I may say) foole, in hope you will deserue it.
what Phisick tooke you, that hath thus restor'd you?
Co: a little sack [and] had power to cure this madnes.
Sis. I hope you are not sober yet, the humour

1756 *not.*] .* 1757 *thinke.*] .* 1771 *rime,*] ,* 1773 *[to]*] single-stroke deletion, Hand 3 *vnto*] interlined above deletion, Hand 3; *to* smudged *[Beggars]*] single-stroke deletion, Hand 3 1774 *feare?*] *?* misformed and joined to [2]*e*; *?* point added*, preceded by Hand 1 point 1775 *businesse,*] ,* 1776 *my*] *m* altered and smudged 1777 *Coaches.*] .* 1783 *breakfast.*] .* 1785 *were*] blot after [2]*e* 1786 *it.*] .* 1787 *you?*] ?* 1788 *[and]*] single-stroke deletion, probably Hand 1 *madnes.*] .*

may change, when you ha slept.
Co: Ile rather stich
my Eyelids vp with Sisters thread, and stare
perpetually.
Sis. then you may see me agen,
Co: I thinke I shannot, vnless it be to wonder
when you are in the Ivie bush. that face?
cut vpon tafata, that creame and prunes? [FOL. 51b]
So many plums in white broth? that scutcheon of
pretence pouderd with ermines? now I looke vpont
\with those black patches it does put me in mind/
[does put me in mind]
of a white soule with sinns vpon't, and frights me.
how sell you grapes? your haire does curle in bunches,
you lipps looke like the Parsons glebe, full of
red, blew, and yellow flowers, how they are chopt
and looke like trenches \made/ to draine the meadowe.
Sis. this rudenes [is beyon]d
is beyond the manners of a gentleman.
Co. I cannot helpe it, and I hope you thinke so.
Sis. I am confirm'd, that now I am forsaken,
but if your Passion haue not drown'd all reason,
I pray let vs part civilly.
Co. withall my hart, I dare then take my leaue to.
Sis. whoe's there?
Co: where.
Sis: behind that tree. [FOL. 52a]
Co: you haue no plott to accuse me for a rape,
'twas at the worst but felony, for cherries
that look'd as [though] they had been a fortnight gather'd.
Sis. I know youle bring me home in Curtesie,
Co: Not I, I wonot trust my selfe, and you
will hardly meet a worse to interrupt you,
fare you well Ladie – do you see that Bull?
Sis. Yes Sir

1790 _you ha slept._] _ou_, _ha_, and _sl_ blotted; .* 1793 _perpetually._] .* 1797 _prunes?_] _?_* 1798 _broth?_] _?_ added* over Hand 1 , 1799 _ermines?_] _?_* 1800] interlined above two carets* 1801 _[does . . . mind]_] deletion hatched over* 1802 _vpon't_] '* _me._] .* 1806 _made_] interlined* _meadowe._] .* 1807 _[is beyon]d_] single-stroke deletion, probably Hand 1 1808 _gentleman._] .* 1812 _civilly._] .* 1813 _to._] .* 1819 _look'd_] _d_ altered from _e_; ' added _[though]_] single-stroke deletion, probably Hand 1 _gather'd._] .*

Co: that is a happie beast,
Sis. [how] \why/ happie Sir.
Co. he writes no Verses to his Mistresse, is
not cosend, nor forsworne to gett her fauour,
bestowes no rings, nor empties his Exchequer
to appeare still in new rich suits, but liues
free, o'the stock of Nature, yet loues none:
Like the great Turke he walkes in his Seraglio,
and doth com̄and which \concubine/ best pleases,
when he has done, he falls to graze, or sleepe, [FOL. 52b]
and wakes, as he had neuer knowne the Dun,
White, Red or brindled Cowe.
Sis. you are vnmanly.
Co: Nay I know you will raile now. I shall like it,
call me a scuruy fellow, proud, and saucie,
an ill bred, crooked Clowne, ile here this rather
then liue vpon your pitty. and yet doe not,
for if you raile too, men that know you can
dissemble, may beleeue you loue me, and
tis not my ayme
Sis. You are a fine Man.
Co. I am in my best cloathes.
Sis. I perceaue
it is truth now, what the world saies of you,
and yet tis strange
Co: 'twere strange it should be otherwise
Sis. you giue your tongue a licence, nor will I hope [FOL. 53a]
your malice should spare me abroad, that haue
so prodigally abus'd a Ladies fame?
that deseru'd nobly from you, but you men
care not whose name you blast with a loose character,
so you maintaine your pride of talke,
Co: howe's this?
it is confess'd I haue talk'd in my tyme,
and talk'd too much; but not too much of you,

1826 *[how]*] single-stroke deletion, probably Hand 1 *why*] interlined above deletion, probably Hand 1 1831 *none:*] :* 1833 *concubine*] interlined above caret* 1836 *brindled*] *l* added *Cowe.*] .* 1845 *Man.*] .* 1848 *now,*] ,* 1849 *and*] blot under *d* 1853 *fame?*] *?* misformed

for I but seldome thought of such a woman
for any other –
Sis. Nay Sir I am satisfied you can talke your pleasure,
Co: haue I not done it too?
Sis. Yes by your owne report, and with a lady,
So much in Vertue and and in birth aboue you;
and therefore I expect not [anie modest language of me].
Co: Stay, this moues [you] me, [FOL. 53b]
I neuer tooke a pleasure yet, to lie
with ladies fames, or euer thought that sport
lay in the tongue, such humo.^{rs} are for men
that liue by brothell offices, let me know
who hath traduc'd me to you thus, he shall
be knowne no more.
Sis. Ile not be guiltie Sir
of any murder, when we meet agen,
and you in better humour, I may tell you,
So farewell Gondarino, nothing's lost,
when you turne woman hater. Exit
Co: She has vext me,
if we two make a Matrimony, after
this rate, the Diuell is like to dance at our wedding. ho?
Enter Deuice
De: hee's here
alo[⟨.⟩]ne too, and the place most opportune, [FOL. 54a]
how shall I beginne – M^{r}. Courtwell – do you loue
any friend of mine?
Co: Not to my knowledge Sir, I should be sorry,
De. Do not you loue a gentlewoman?
Co. if she be a friend of yours, ile take the first
occasion, to neglect her for your sake.
De. It will become your wisdome, and your safety,
Co: what mischiefe haue done to your face?
De. My face?
Co: You looke so scuruily, come hither, thou

1863 *too?*] ?* 1866 *[anie . . . me]*] hatched over* 1867 *[you]*] single-stroke deletion*, ? Hand 3 *me,*] added*, ? Hand 3 1873 *more.*] .* 1877 *Gondarino*] *i* double dotted *lost,*] ,* 1880 *two*] *w* altered* from *o* *Matrimony,*] *i* dotted*, preceded by Hand 1 dot; ,* 1881 *rate,*] ,* 1882 *Deuice*] *i* dotted*, preceding Hand 1 dot 1884 *alo[⟨.⟩]ne*] *a* added*; deletion* 1886 *mine?*] ?* 1892 *face?*] ?* 1893 *face?*] ?* 1894 *come*] *o* blotted

New Monster with more feet then a Caterpiller,
what tyme a day ist? you that move vpon
So many wheeles, say Monsier, are you not
a walkeing Clock? I haue a mighty minde,
to see you tooke a peeces.
De. I doe not like this,
you wonot put me Sir together againe, [Fol. 54b]
Co: I wonot take the paines, why do you smile now?
De. at your conceit, to thinke I was a Clock,
I am a watch I neuer strike, hee's valiant.
Co. you haue pretty colours there, are these yo[r] Mistresses?
De. if you did know the mistery, you would applaud 'em
haue you read liure de blason? what meane you?
Co: I will bestow 'em Sir vpon some forehorse,
they will become a Countrey teame rarely,
De Mor blew!
why you dare fight it seemes, and I was told
you were no Cauellier, a very dreame,
a wedg for men to breake their swords vpon,
I shall neuer trust fame agen, for your sake,
Co: thou neuer cosendst me,
De. I was neuer so illiterate in man,
Co: for I did euer thinke thou durst not fence,
but
but at a Complement, a glittering vapour [Fol. 55a]
a thing of clothes, and fitt for chambermaides
to whet their witts vpon, but now resolue
either to haue your skin flead of, or fight wo'me
for troubling my present meditations.
De Why Sir, if you be serious, I shall quit
that preiudice you haue vpon my valo[r],
looke you Sir I can draw, and thus prouok'd,
I dare chastise you too; Cause I was merry,
I am not bound to feed your spleene eternally
with laughter. Yet I am not ignorant

1896 *ist?*] ?* 1898 *Clock?*] ? added*, preceding Hand 1 , *minde,*] ,* 1904 *valiant.*] .* 1906 *'em*] *e* altered * 1908 *forehorse,*] ,* 1909 *rarely,*] ,* 1913 *vpon,*] ,* 1914 *sake,*] ,* 1915 *me,*] ,* 1916 *man,*] *m* blotted; ,* 1917 *fence,*] ,* 1917a *but*] *b* smudged 1921 *of,*] otiose point after , , ?* 1922 *meditations.*] .* 1925 *prouok'd*] *d* altered from *e*

what an aduantage Sir your weapon giues you
in length.
Co: Wee'le change, why this is hono^{r} in thee.
they measure and Deuice getts both weapons
De Now Sir keepe of.
Co: th'art not so base.
De. I neuer cosen'd you, do you remember? [FOL. 55b]
these two will guide me on the rope.
Co. you meane to dance then.
De. Yes the Canaries, but with quicker tyme
then you I hope can follow, thus I begin.
fa la la &c – Excurrit
Co: what a heathen Coward's this, [how the]
how the rogue tripps like a fairie to y^{e} towne w^{t}h 'em, he has \been/
a footman sure, I haue not aire enough to ouertake
him, and twill be darke presently, if I loose the sight
on him, ile search y^{e} towne and if I find him not there,
pursue him with hue and cries, and after hang him.
Exit
Enter S^{r}. Francis a taper prepar'd
Fr: the Sun̄, whose busie eye is still employ'd
a spie vpon our actions, tir'd with waiting,
is
is drowsie gone to bed, about whose pillow [FOL. 56a]
Night hath hung all her wings, and set vp tapers,
as if the Day were tymerous like a Child,
and must haue lights to sleepe by. welcome all
the houres that gouerne pleasure, but be slow
when you haue blest me with my wishes, Time
and loue should dwell like twins, make this yor bower,
and charme the aire to sweetnes, and to silence.
fauour me now, and you shall change your states,
Tyme shall be old no more, I will contract
with Destiny, if he will spare his winges,
to giue him youth, and beauty, that we may

1931 *thee.*] .* 1933 *of.*] .* 1935 *remember?*] ?* 1936 *rope.*] .* 1937 *then.*] .* 1939 *begin.*] .* 1941 *[how the]*] single-stroke deletion, probably Hand 1 1942 *been*] interlined above caret 1943 *sure,*] ,* 1944 *presently,*] ,* 1945 *there,*] ,* 1946 *pursue*] ^{I}*u* altered from *e* *him.*] .*, preceded by Hand 1 . 1954 *by.*] .* 1958 *sweetnes,*] ,* *silence.*] .* 1961 *winges,*] ,* 1962 *youth,*] ,*

find euery minute a fresh child of pleasure.
Loue shall be proud to be no more a boy,
but grow to perfect strength, and bold consistence,
for when two Actiue Louers meet, so happie
as wee, whose equall flames light to embraces,
'twill
'twill be no weight, to number many yeares [FOL. 56b]
in our delights, and thinke all age a blessing.
but language is to narrow, to expresse
what I expect, tis fitt my soule retire,
till she present her selfe, and if it can
Measure my hop'd for ioyes with thought, prepare
to entertaine the happines. Ex.

S^{r}. Richard and his Lady abed. Enter
Dorothy with a Light.

Do. I haue set already my designe a moueing,
to take my Captaine Vnderwit, who in wine
was late more feirce vpon me. I'th meane tyme,
I cannot choose but laugh, at the deuice
wee haue to cheat my Master, sure the Diuell
is a great friend to women, that loue men,
he doth so furnish vs with quaint inventions,
presently after supper, she began
her
her fitt o'the toothach, and did counterfeit [FOL. 57a]
so naturally, but since she went to bed
She almost rau'd by turnes, I heare her at it

la: Oh – oh, whoe's there?

Do: tis I forsooth, I heard you groane, and I
haue not the hart to sleepe, shall I watch by you?

la. Oh no no no, get you to bed, make fast the chamber
I cannot endure the Candle.

Dorothy towards the dore putts out
the Candle and returnes

S^{r}. R: Deare hart be patient,

1963 *pleasure.*] .* 1964 *boy,*] ,* 1965 *strength,*] ,* 1967 *wee,*] ,* 1967a *'twill (tw'ill)*] *t* added; *i* altered from *l* 1968 *weight,*] ,* 1969 *blessing.*] .* 1971 *expect,*] ,* *retire,*] ,* 1973 *hop'd*] *'d* altered* from e *thought*] ^{2}*t* added* 1978 *Vnderwit,*] ,* 1979 *tyme,*] ,* 1980 *laugh,*] ,* 1982 *women,*] ,* *men,*] ,* 1983 *inventions,*] ,* 1984 *supper,*] ,* 1987 *turnes*] *s* blotted *I . . . it*] ? added Hand 1 1992 *Candle.*] .* 1993 *putts*] *s* added*

la: I, you haue your homilies of Patience, but if you had my
paine twould make you wild, oh.

Sr. R: Ile send for the french toothdrawer in the morning,

la: Oh there is no rack, nor torture like it, what shall I doe?
I shall neuer sleepe agen,

Sr. R: which tooth ist?

Do: the sweet one you may be sure, that troubles her, [Fol. 57b]

la: this this, o that, there –

Ri: they are happie that are old, and haue no teeth,

la: Oh, take heed, now it shoots vp to my head.

Ri: thou dost make my head ake with the noise.

la: if you knew what I suffer, yor head would ake indeed,

[Ri]: I must rise, and walke in the Chamber, there is no remedy

Ri: you will catch more cold.

La: Oh no no deere life do not crosse me, and you were in my
torment, you would rise, and trie any thing for a litle ease,
It cannot be worse, the paine sure came with a cold, and who
knowes but an other cold may cure me

Ri. I prethe come to bed agen

la: So so, do=not troble me I am now in some litle ease,
its a heauenly thing to be goeing

Ri. Dost heare?

la. yor Noise will bring my paine back agen, if you knew what
a
a vexation it were for me to speake, you wo'not put me too't [Fol. 58a]
so, if you doe talke I wonot answere a word more, oh

Ri: \well/ by this no light ile to London tomorrow.

she takes Dorothy by the hand [to] exit

now do I see it is possible that a womans teeth should
be as troublesome as her tongue.

Do. oh oh

Ri: I cannot choose but pitty her, that any woman should hold
so much paine in a hollow tooth.

Do: if my Mr. touched with so much compassion should rise, and
force me to bed to him, I must not cry out a rape, tis at the

1996 *I,*] ,* 1997 *paine*] *i* dotted*, preceding Hand 1 dot *wild,*] ,* *oh.*] .*, preceded by Hand 1 . 1998 *morning,*] ,* 1999 *doe?*] ?* 2001 *ist?*] ?* 2005 *head.*] .* 2006 *noise.*] .* 2008 *[Ri]:*] single-stroke deletion, probably Hand 1 *Chamber,*] ,* 2011 *rise,*] ,* 2012 *worse,*] ,* *cold,*] , marked twice 2021 *well*] interlined above caret 2022 *[to]*] single-stroke deletion 2024 *tongue.*] .*, preceded by Hand 1 . 2028 *if*] *i* dotted* 2029 *him,*] ,*

worst on my side but fornication in my owne defence,
Ri. I prethe come to Bed,
Do. oh; oh; oh,
Ri. the musick at a conuocation of Catts vpon a witches vpsitting
is the spheres to this Catterwalling, I will thrust my head into
the Pillow as Dametas did in a bush, when the beare was a
comeing; and then I shanot heare her. /
Do: Oh – this is a kind of Purgatory for sin̄s of the flesh, [FOL. 58b]
if she should fall asleepe with ye tother kn^{t}., it is not
possible I should hold out till morning, that which would fright
away an Ague hath put me into a feare, I shall ha the
toothache indeed with counterfeiting, I haue
knowne some men haue caught the stammers so, my gum̄s
begin to murmure, there is a feare all ouer my flesh
she will stay so long, and then –
S^{r}. Ri: coughs – uh uh
Do: Oh oh,
ile shift places to shew more distraction, at the worst
my noise shall be within his reach, it may giue her
notice to returne too Exit
S^{r}. Francis asleepe, a table inke and
Paper. Enter Lady.
la: I am full of feares, and my owne motion frights me,
this furious loue is a strange Pilot, Sir,
where are you? ha? asleepe, can any dulnes
that
that is not Death, possess a gentleman, [FOL. 59a]
So valiant in desires, when he expects
to meete his Mistresse? how I blush to raise him,
was I not worth thy wa[it]king expectation?
farwell, yet something that a cha[r]ine that's fastned
to my poore hart restraines me, Inke and paper
Ile leaue him a short monument of this shame
and my neglected loue: – Writes
he knowes my hand, farwell forgetfull Louer?

2030 *defence,*] ,* 2031 *Bed,*] ,* 2035 *Dametas*] ^{1}*a* altered* from *e* *beare*] *e* interlined above caret* 2036 *her.*] .*, above Hand 1. 2037 *flesh,*] ,* 2051 *Paper.*] .*, above Hand 1. *Lady.*] .* 2052 *feares,*] ,* *frights*] *i* dotted * *me,*] ,* 2057 *Mistresse?*] ?*, above Hand 1, *him,*] ,* 2058 *wa[it]king*] deleted*; *k* altered* from *e* *expectation?*] ?* 2059 *cha[r]ine* *in* altered* from *m*

Fra: What? haue I slept? some witchcraft did betray [me out]
my eyes to so much darkenes, yet my dreame
was full of rapture, such, as I, with all
my wakeing sence would flie to meet, me thought
I saw a thousand Cupids slide from heauen,
and landing here, made this their scene of reuells,
Clapping their golden feathers, which kept tyme,
while their owne feet strook musike to their dance,
as
as they had trod, and touched so many lutes. [FOL. 59b]
This done, within a Cloud formd like a Throne,
She (to whome loue had consecrate this night
my Mistress) did descend and comeing toward me,
my soule that euer wakes, angrie to see
My body made a Prisoner, and so mock'd,
shooke of the chaines of sleepe, least I should loose
essentiall pleasure for a dreame. Tis happie
I will not trust my selfe with ease and and silence,
but walke and waite her comeing, y^t must bless me.
forgiue me you bright starrs, and do not frowne
that I haue not attended, as became
one, that must liue by your kind influence.
Not yet appeard; she did comand I should
with confidence expect her, ha? what's here?
this Character was not visible before.
That man's too much compos'd of phleame /reades/ [FOL. 60a]
will loose his Mistress for a Dreame
Tis hers, I know't, she has been here, oh fatall!
and finding me asleepe scorn'd to vncharme
my dull and cursed silence, this distracts me,
haue I so long, with so much Art and study
labour'd this hono^r, and obtaind what my
Ambition look'd at, her consent, and when
the tree it selfe bowd downe its golden fruit,
and [ex]tempted me to gather, must I make

2064 *[me out]*] double-stroke deletion 2066 *such,*] ,* 2068 *heauen,*] ,* 2069 *reuells,*] ,* 2070 *tyme,*] ,* 2072 *lutes.*] .* 2073 *Throne,*] ,* 2079 *essentiall*] *ia* altered from *u* *dreame.*] .*, above Hand 1 . 2080 *silence,*] ,* 2081 *me.*] .* 2084 *kind*] *i* dotted twice *influence.*] *i* dotted*, preceded by Hand 1 dot; .* 2086 *here?*] ?* 2087 *Character*] *c* altered from *r* *before.*] .*; otiose stroke above. 2088 *compos'd*] ^{2}*o* blotted */reades/*] added*, Hand 3 2097 *and*] added*, ? Hand 3 *[ex]tempted*] deleted*; ^{1}*t* added*

my selfe vncap[e]able and be guilty of
so black, so base a forfeit? I could teare
My Eyelids of, that durst let in a Mist
so darke, and so destroying, must I sleepe
at such a tyme, that the Diuell must be ouer
watche too? This houre hath blasted such a hope,
as the Earth neuer teem'd with, nor the spring
gaue vp in smileing blosomes to the breath [Fol. 60b]
of those sweet windes, that whisper from the West
A tale of triumph to the yeere, I could
dissolue with curseing of my Lethargie,
how shall I looke vpon her face? whose loue
and bold aduenture I haue thus rewarded?
but passion wonot cure my wound, which must
bleed, till I see her, and then, either cease
blest by her pardon, or dismiss a life
(though iust) too poore a Sacrifice for her anger.
Where shall I hide my selfe and shame foreuer. /
Exit. /

The Fift Act:

Enter Sister.

Sis. I cannot forgett my carelesse gentleman,
his neglect, and reproaches haue wrought strangly [Fol. 61a]
vpon me – hee's here. Enter Courtwell
Co: is there not a weesill crept into your Chamber lady?
Sis. A weesill Sir?
Co. A Mounsier suckegge.
Sis. do you take my Chamber for a henns neast?
Co. there is a thing, that calls himselfe Device,
one, that will break the hart of a Post horse
to continue a hand gallop with him, yo[r] Alamode
your fighting faery feather'd footed seruant –
when saw you him?
Sis. My fighting seruant? has he beaten you sir?
perhapps he thought you were his Riuall, surely,

2098 *vncap[e]able*] deleted* 2100 *of,*] ,* 2103 *too?*] ?* *hope,*] ,* 2105 *blosomes*] *m* second minim blotted 2106 *West*] *W* altered* from *r* 2108 *Lethargie,*] ,* 2109 *how*] *o* blotted *face?*] ? added above Hand 1 , 2110 *rewarded?*] ? point missing 2112 *then,*] ,* 2114 *anger.*] .* 2117 *Fift*] *F* and *f* retraced 2118 *Sister.*] .* 2119 *gentleman,*] ,* 2120 *neglect,*] ,* *reproaches*] *c* altered from *a* 2122 *weesill*] [2]*e* altered 2126 *thing,*] ,* *Device,*] ,* 2131 *seruant?*] ? added* above Hand 1 , 2132 *his*] *i* blotted

I saw him not since yesterday,
Co. bu'y Ladie – how many mile ist to the next Cutlers?
the rogue has pawn'd, or sold my sword.
Offers to goe forth
Sis. Dee heare sir? [FOL. 61b]
I can tell you now, what lady 'twas, you did abuse so.
Co: I abuse a Ladie? tell me the slaue
reported it, I hope twill proue this Mounsier,
if ere wee meet agen. who wast?
Sis. Vpon condition Sir, you will requite me,
but with one gentle fauour
Co. Any thing –
Sis You must sitt downe, and heare me then, while I
at a distance thus deliuer –
Co. tis more state.
Sis. I am most vnfortunate.
Co. In what deare Damsell?
Sis and much wrongd by a gentleman I lou'd,
Co. Can he be a gentlemen that dares
wrong so much loue and beauty? what's ye offence?
Sis. he wonot loue agen,
Co. and you would haue [FOL. 62a]
the stubborne man corrected?
Sis I would be
reuengd, if I knew how, and hono^{r} him
should do me Iustice,
Co. Name the man, Ile doot,
Sis. I cannot.
Co. how?
Sis. Yet turne yor face, alas it is your selfe,
I haue your word to punish him,
Co: Sweet Ladie,
I am well acquainted with the worthy gentleman,
but will nor kill, nor strike him, for I know
he has iust reason not to loue you – you

2133 *yesterday,*] ,* 2134 *bu'y*] '* *Cutlers?*] ? point added*, preceded by Hand 1 . 2135 *pawn'd,*] ,* lines 2137–2205 bracketed 2138 *now,*] ,* *'twas,*] ,* 2141 *agen.*] .* 2142 *me,*] ,* 2145 *must*] *st* blotted *downe,*] ,* *then,*] ,* 2147 *more*] *o* altered from *y* *state.*] .* 2148 *vnfortunate.*] .* 2149 *Damsell?*] ?* 2152 *offence?*] ?* 2153 *agen,*] ,*, preceding Hand 1 . 2157 *how,*] ,* 2158 *Iustice,*] ,* 2162 *selfe,*] ,* 2163 *him,*] ,* 2164 *Ladie,*] ,* 2165 *gentleman,*] ,* 2166 *kill,*] ,* *him,*] ,*, preceded by Hand 1,

of all your sex, he told me so.
Sis. his reason –
Co: was in these wordes, suppose you heare him speake it,
now do you sit – Lady when I consider you, [FOL. 62b]
the perfect frame of what we can call hansome,
with all your attributes of soule and body,
where no addition, or de[s]traction, can
by Cupids nicer Crittick find a fault,
Or Mercury with your eternall flame,
and then consider, what a thing I am,
to this high Character of you, so low,
so lost to noble merits, I despaire
to loue a Mistresse, cannot loue agen,
Sis. this is a much dissembled Modesty,
Co. therefore giue me the kinder Chambermaid,
that will returne me loue for my two peeces,
and giue me back twelue pennyworth agen,
which is as much, as I can well receaue,
So there is thirty, \and/ nyne shillings cleere
gotten in Loue and much good do her wo't,
I thinke it \very/ well bestow'd.
Sis. but if I thinke you worthy, and accept [FOL. 63a]
your seruice, it destroies this other reason
for your despaire, why I can praise you too,
Co. No, lett it alone, I haue other reasons Lady
among my papers, \but/ to loue, or to be in loue,
is to be guld, that's the plaine English of Cupids latine,
beside all reuerence to the calling, I
haue vou'd neuer to marry, and you know
Loue may bring a Man toot at last, and therfore my fine
Gewgaw do not abuse me.
Sis. how can I, when you will neither loue, nor marry me?
Co. I was not made for a husband,
Sis but I would make you,
Co. I know what you would make me.
Enter Seruant

2168 *so.*] .*, preceded by Hand 1 . 2170 *wordes,*] ,* 2171 *sit*] *i* added* 2172 *the*] *he* added* below Hand 1 ' 2174 *de[s]traction*] *e* altered* from *i*; *[s]* deleted* 2175 *Crittick*] ^{1}*t* altered *fault,*] ,* 2176 *flame,*] ,* 2177 *consider,*] ,* 2178 *you,*] ,* *low,*] ,* 2180 *agen,*] ,* 2181 *dissembled*] ^{2}*s* altered from *c* *Modesty,*] ,* 2182 *me*] *m* altered* from *on* *Chambermaid,*] ,*, preceded by Hand 1 , 2183 *peeces,*] ,* 2184 *pennyworth*] ^{2}*n* first minim altered 2185 *much,*] ,* 2186 *and*] interlined above caret* 2188 *very*] interlined above caret*, Hand 3 *bestow'd.*] .*, preceded by Hand 1 . 2189 *if*] *i* added* *accept*] *ac* altered* from *ex* 2190 *it . . . reason*] added*, ? Hand 3 2191 *despaire,*] ,* , preceding Hand 1. 2193 *but*] interlined* 2194 *latine,*] ,* 2198 *me.*] . marked twice* 2199 *me?*] ?* 2202 *me.*] .*

Ser: Mounsier Deuice if you be alone, would present
his seruice. /
Co: Is he come? [Fol. 63b]
Sis. Sir do \me/ but one fauour, ile recant
My Loue, I wonot haue so much as one
good thought on you, I will neglect you, sir,
Nay and abuse you too, if you obscure [bu]
but for three minutes
Co. Ile haue patience so long.
Sis. Admitt him – I wilbe reueng'd o somebody.
Now sir Enter Deuice
De. I ha brought you a weapon Lady –
la: Mee, what to do sir?
De. tis Iustice I present it to your feete,
whose loue arme me to vindicate yor hono^{r},
Sis. My honor?
De this is but the first of my valour in your cause,
if you affect these Monuments, ile make
you vp an Armorie, meane tyme receaue
my
My Seruice with this sword, if he prouoke me [Fol. 64a]
to fight with him agen, Ile cut his hand of
and bring [it] \that/ wo'me to present the next.
Sis. whose hand deare seruant?
De. he is not worth the nameing, la's this does not
deserue your knowledge, only thinke what I
dare do, when your bright name is question'd,
and I in tyme, may merit to be cald
the darling of your Virgin thoughts
Sis: I pray stay
my name traduc'd, who was so impudent?
do me the grace to let me know, on whome
your Valo^{r} had been exercis'd.
De. why the formall thing – Courtwell I would call him
gentleman, but that I ha' baffled him

2206 *come?*] ?* 2207 *me*] interlined above caret* 2210 *[bu]*] single-stroke deletion 2212 *long.*] .* 2214 *sir*] *i* dotted* 2217 *feete*] ^{1}*e* retraced*; ^{2}*e* altered from *a* 2221 *affect*] *a* blotted 2222 *Armorie,*] ,* 2225 *that*] interlined above deletion* *next.*] .* 2226 *deare*] *a* blotted 2229 *bright*] *i* dotted*, preceded by Hand 1 dot

you need no other witnes, but his sword
with that fine holliday hilt Ladie
She shutts the Doore
Sis. Looke you sir, I ha made fast the Doore, [Fol. 64b]
because I meane before you goe, to haue
a satisfaction, for the base Iniury,
you ha done me.
De I done you Iniurie?
Sis. Not that I value Courtwell, whome you would
pretend has been to saucy with my hono^{r},
but cause I scorne to owne a goodnes, should
depend vpon your sword, or vindication,
Ile fight with you my selfe, in this small voll[o]ume,
against your bulke in folio.
Co: Excellent wench!
De: I was your Champion lady.
Sis. Ide rather haue no fame, then heare thee name it.
thou[g] fight for a Ladies hono^{r}, and disarme
a gentleman? thou fence before the pageants,
and make roome for the Porters, when like Elephants
they carry once a yeare the Citty Castles,
or
or goe a feasting with the Drum, and footboyes [Fol. 65a]
to the Bankeside, and saue the Beares a whipping
that day, thou art cudgeld, for thy saucy challenging
a serieant with one eye, that was too much too,
come Sir I meane to haue a bout with you
De. at that weapon?
Sis. this and no other
De Ile rather bleed to death, then lift a sword
in my defence, whose inconsiderate brightnes
may fright the Roses from your cheeke, and leaue
the Lillies to lament the rude divorce.
but were a Man to dare me, and your enemy
my rage more nimble, then Median shaft

2243 *satisfaction,*] , * 2244 *me.*] .* 2250 *in*] *i* dotted*, preceded by Hand 1 dot *voll[o]ume,*] *u* interlined above deletion* 2251 *folio.*] .* 2252 *wench!*] *!* point added* 2253 *lady.*] .* 2254 *fame,*] ,* 2262 *too,*] ,* 2269 *divorce.*] .*

should flie into his bosome, and your eye
change anger into smiles, to see me fight,
and cut him into a ragged staffe

Enter Courtwell

Co. I can hold no longer.
you haue gott a stomack Sir with running, ile trie [Fol. 65b]
hou you can eate a sword.
De. ha you an ambush lady Ile cry out murder,
is two to one faire play?
Co: let me cut one legg of, to marre his runing,
De: hold let me speake.
Co: what canst thou say for thy basenes?
De: some men loues wit, and can without dishono^{r}
endure a ieast, why do you thinke I know not
you were here, and but obscur'd to see my humo^{r},
I came to waite vpon you with your sword, I.
Co. how came you by'te, confesse before this Lady.
De: Dost thinke her witt's so limber, to beleeue
I could compell it from thee, twas a trick
a meere conceipt of mirth, thou sha't ha mine,
dost thinke I stand vpon a sword? Ile gi' thee
a case of Pistolls when we come to London,
and shoot me when I loue thee not, pox ont,
thou apprehende'st me well enough.
Co. but I am not [Fol. 66a]
satisfied, do you affect this gentlewoman?
De. hum?
Co. you will resolue sir?
De. as may become a stranger, ile not loose
thy friendship for all woman kind.
Co. he dares not owne you –
Sis. I easilie forgiue him, I should hate
my selfe, if I depended on his pitty,
Co: th'art a noble wench, shall we leaue of
these Iigs, and speake our harts in earnest, by

2273 *smiles,*] ,* 2276 *longer.*] .* 2277 *you*] *y* tail smudged 2279 *murder,*] ,* 2280 *play?*] ?, preceding .* 2281 *of,*] ,* 2282 *speake.*] .* 2284 *without*] *o* blotted 2286 *humo^{r},*] ,*, preceded by ,* 2287 *I.*] .* 2288 *by'te,*] ,* 2289 *limber,*] ,* *Lady.*] .* 2294 *ont,*] , above , 2299 *will*] *i* dotted* 2301 *kind.*] .* 2306 *earnest,*] ,*, preceded by Hand 1 ,; otiose mark above *t*

these twin lips, I loue thee extreamely,
Sis Sweare by your owne,
Co. they shall bee mine,
Mounsier for your penance, you shall along and witnes.
Sis. what I pray?
Co. the Priest shall tell you, come we haue both dissembled, [Fol. 66b]
we do loue one another
Sis. tis not possible,
Co: Vnless you will denie me i'the Church,
I ha vou'd to lie with you tonight Deuice
amble before, and find the Parson out,
we will bee friends, and thou shalt be her father,
2. De. I must maintaine my humour or be beaten, ex.
Co: come, weele haue no more acquainted –
Sis. very pretty,
I may deceaue you yet, for all your confidence.
Co: if the skie fall, weele haue the Larkes to supper
2 Exeunt

Enter Ladie S^r^. Francis Dorothy

la: It was strange neglect Sir.
Fr: I confesse it,
and not deserue to liue for't, yet if you
but knew my suffrings. /
la: let her be Iudge. [Fol. 67a]
Fr: by no meanes Madam.
la: you may trust her knowledge.
Fr: this is worse then a whipping now, these Ladies
haue no mercy on a Delinquent, I must stand toot.
there is no tyrant to a Chamber woman,
made Iudg in such a Cause, Ide giue a limbe
to be quit now, but if she choose, I am
a Criple for this world.
Do: Ist possible a Man and such a beast?
Fr. So, I must to \the/ shameles –
la: what punishment can be equall to the offence?
Do. he lookes with some Compunction for his fault,

2307 *extreamely,*] ,* 2308 *owne,*] ,* 2309 *mine,*] ,* 2314 *possible,*] ,* 2315 *i'the*] *i* dotted* *Church,*] ,*, preceded by Hand 1 , 2317 *before,*] ,* *out,*] ,* 2318 *friends,*] ,* *father,*] ,* 2319 *beaten,*] ,* 2326 *Sir.*] .* 2327 *it,*] ,* 2330 *Iudge.*] *e* added*; .* 2331 *Madam.*] .* 2332 *knowledge.*] .* above Hand 1 , 2340 *So,*] ,* *to*] altered* from *be* *the*] interlined above caret* 2341 *offence?*] ?* 2342 *Compunction*] *C* retraced *fault,*] ,*

troth Madam choose an other night, and trye,
whether he will sleepe agen
Fr. Mercifull wench!
if we peece agen, it shall be a good turne in thy way.
la: My husband is this day resolu'd for London, [FOL. 67b]
it is his humour, or els worse, suspition.
ther's no pretence for him to stay behind,
Do: you haue made ill vse of your time S^{r}. Francis,
I know not how to helpe you, Seauen yeare hence,
you may haue such an other oportunitie.
la: watch if my husband come not this way Dorothy,
well sir, though your transgresse deserue no pardon,
yet I am charitable, vpon Condition –
Fr. Any thing Madam, this shewes exlent in you,
No pennance shall displease, so you absolue me,
bid me to clime some Rock, or Pyramide,
vpon whose narrow spire, you haue aduanc'd
my Peace, and I will reach it, or else fall
lost to the world in my attempt.
la: you speake gloriously, the condition that assures
your pardon's only this, that you conclude,
here
here all your loose desires, with a resolue [FOL. 68a]
neuer to prosecute, or hope to enioy me.
Fr: Call you this Charity? let me rather loose
your pardon, then for euer to be thus forfeited,
bind me neuer to see you (and yet that
were Cruelty) then charme me to forgett
that I am man, or haue a hart, and you
a beauty, which your absence, can as well
make nothing, as deuide from my adoreing,
it is not cure, but killing to prescribe
I neuer must enioy you, if you haue
resolu'd a Death vpon me, lett it bee
when we like Louers haue embrac'd –

2343 *night,*] ,* *trye,*] ,* 2348 *suspition.*] .* 2352 *oportunitie.*] .* 2356 *Madam,*] ,* 2361 *attempt.*] .* 2364 *desires,*] ,* above Hand 1 , 2365 *me.*] .* 2372 *adoreing,*] ,*

la: it is not possible
Fr: Nothing in loue can be impossible to willing mindes,
Ile tell you Madam – Sure the Diuell has
forsworne the flesh – there may be a plot – I haue it,
an
an exelent rare deuise if you but fauour it, [FOL. 68b]
your husband is imediatly for London,
I must in modesty ride with him, you
are left behind.
la: how can that profitt you?
Do: what a deale of submission these foolish men
trouble vs women with, that are more forward
to be friendes agen, \then/ they are
Fr: I will counterfeit a fall.
la: a fall?
Fr: I, from my horse, obserue me then –
Do: My confederate I hope by this tyme is at gate,
enquiring for Sir Richard very formally,
from the old knight his Master, and good ladie,
the fellow has witt to manage it,
Fr: My footman shall pretend himselfe the Surgeon to,
attend me, is't not rare?
Stand but to'th fate of this, and if it faile, [FOL. 69a]
I will sitt downe a Convert, and renounce
all wanton hope hereafter, deerest Madam,
if you did meane before this honour to me,
lett not your loving thoughts freeze in a Minuit,
My genius is a prophet.
Do: S^{r}. Richard Madam
is comeing this way,
Fr. shall I hope agen?
la: I wo'not say you shall despaire, –
Fr: you blesse me. Exit
Do: My busines is afoote, your Iewell Madam
will credit much the cause,

2384 *behind.*] .* 2388 *then*] interlined above caret*, Hand 3 2393 *enquiring*] *u* second minim and *i* base retraced* *formally,*] ,*, preceded by Hand 1 , 2405 *way,*] , preceding . 2408 *Exit*] *E* retraced after false start

la. Wee will withdraw, and lett me know how you haue cast ye plott
Exeunt

Enter S^{r}. Richard opening a Letter
a footman waiting. /

Ri: from thy Master? his name.
Foo: S^{r}. Walter Littleland. [FOL. 69b]
Ri: I doe not know him.
Foo. his name is well knowne in Lincolnsheire neere the fenns,
there were his family antient gentlemen before the
Conquest, some say euer since the flood.
Ri: Littleland?
foo: but he has now more land then three of the best in ye shi[e]re
thanke the Duchmen, that haue drunk vp all the water.
Ri: they water drinkers?
foo: why not, as well as eate dry land, they are lin'd with butter
Sir, and feare no dropsie

S^{r}. Richard reades.

She has been absent theis two yeares, the occasion her
dislike and disaffection to a gentleman, whome, I confesse
I did too seueerely urge her to marry, if she haue
livd with you, as my late intelligence hath enformed me,
in the nature of a seruant, which is beneath my wishes,
and her condition, I hope, vpon this knowledge, you
will
will with consideration of her quality (she being [FOL. 70a]
the onely Child and heire to my fortune) vse her
like a gentlewoman? And though my yeares haue made
me vnfitt for trauell, I do intend vpon returne of yor
Letters, personally to giue you thankes for yor respects
to my Daughter, whome I shall receaue as new blessing
from you, and be happie vpon any turne presented to
expresse my selfe for your fauours, your true
friend and seruant W: Litleland.
My maide Dorothy a knights Daughter and heire?
doe you know your yong Mistresse?

2415 *name.*] . preceded by . following Hand 1 dot; deletion* 2420 *flood.*] .* 2421 *Littleland?*] ?* 2422 *foo:*] ^{1}*o* blotted *shi[e]re*] *i* dotted* 2423 *Duchmen,*] ,* *vp*] *v* altered 2425 *dry land*] *d* and *d* ascenders smudged 2442 *Litleland.*] .* 2443 *maide*] *e* ? added* *heire?*] ?*

Fo: I shall be happie to see her, and present her with a Letter, &
some token from her Ladie Mother.
Ri. I pray trust me to deliuer it.
foo: with all my hart Sir you may comand. Enter Thomas
Ri: Thomas pray entertaine this footman in the butterie,
Let him drinke and refresh himselfe, and set the cold
chine of Beefe before him –
he has ranne hard
Tho: that will stay his stomack indeed, but Claret is your only [FOL. 70b]
binder,
Fo: Sack while you liue after a heat sir,
Tho: Please you my friend ile shew you the way to be drunke,
Exit.
Ri: To my louing Daughter. May not this be a trick?
by your fauour Madam. – he opens the Letter.
Enter Vnderwit
Captaine, gather you the sence of that Letter,
while I peruse this, you know Mistress Dorothy.
Vn. I haue had a great desire to know her I confess, but
she is still like the bottome of the Map terra incognita
I haue been a long tyme houering about ye Magellan
Streights, but haue made no new discoueries,
Ri: ha? this is not counterfeit, I dare trust my owne Iudgment
tis a very rich one, I am confirmd, and will seale
them vp agen, my Ladies woman S^{r}. Walter Litlelands
Daughter and heire? what thinke you now of M^{ris}. Dorothy?
Vn. a great deale better then I did, and yet I haue lou'd her
this
this halfe yeare in a [way] kind of way, o'my conscience why [FOL. 71a]
may not I marry her?
Ri: this Iewell was sent by her mother to her.
Vn: Deere Vncle conseale 'till I haue talk'd with her, oh
for some witchcraft to make all sure.
Ri: I like this well, shees here –
Enter Dorothy
Vn. I vow, M^{ris}. Dorothy if I were immodest, 'twas the

2445 *her,*] ,* 2446 *Mother.*] .* 2447 *it.*] .* 2448 *comand.*] .* preceding Hand 1 , 2454 *binder,*] ,* 2455 *sir,*] ,* 2456 *drunke,*] ,* 2461 *Letter,*] ,* 2462 *Dorothy.*] .* 2465 *Magellan*] *e* altered 2466 *discoueries,*] ,* 2472 *[way]*] single-stroke deletion 2474 *her.*] .* 2476 *sure.*] .*

meere impudence of my sack, and not my owne disposition,
but if you please to accept my loue now, by the way
of Marriage, I will make you satisfaction like a
gentleman, in the point of hono^{r}.
Do: your birth and estate is to high, and vnequall for me Sir,
Vn. what care I for a portion or a face, she that has
good eyes has good – give me vertue.
Do. you are pleas'd to make your mirth of me,
Vn. by this Rubie, nay you shall weare it in ye broad eye of the
world, dost thinke I am in Ieast?
Do. Sir Richard – [Fol. 71b]
Vn. and he were tenn S^{r}. Richards, I am out of my wardship,
Do. how he flutters in the lime bush, it takes rarely,
Vn. what a necessary thing now, were a household
Chaplaine? Ext
Ri. So, so, the wench inclines, I will hasten my Iourney, that
I may appeare with more excuse, when they are
married in my absence.

Enter Captaine and Engine

Cap. Sir I heare you are for London presentlie,
it will concerne you, take this gentleman
along w'ee, to bee cur'd,
Ri. M^{r}. Engine sick.
Cap: Oh Sir dangerously, he has purg'd his Stomack, but ye ill
spiritts are flowne into his head, and spoild his eares.
he was euer troubled with Deuices in his head,
I stronglie feare he must haue his scull open'd,
his braines are very foule within, I know [Fol. 72a]
and can direct you, to an ex'lent Surgeon
En: I cannot heare you Captaine –
Ca: one that has a rare dexteritie, at lanceing
or opening of a stomack that has crudities,
So neat at seperation of a limbe,
and quartering of treason –
Ri: You meane the hangman?

2483 *hono^{r}.*] .* 2484 *Sir,*] ,* 2486 *vertue.*] .* 2487 *me,*] ,* 2492 *rarely,*] ,* 2501 *cur'd,*] ,* 2502 *sick.*] .* 2503 *Stomack*] *S* altered 2511 *crudities,*] ^{1}*i* dotted*, preceded by Hand 1 dot; ^{2}*i* added*; ,* 2512 *limbe,*] ,* 2514 *hangman?*] ?*

Ca: he has practised late to mend his hand, and now
with the very wind and florish of his Instrument,
he will strike flatt a Proiector at twelue score.
Ri: Does he not heare you?
Ca: he has lost that sence he saies, vnless he counterfeits,
it wilbe your securitie to see him
safe in the Surgeons hands. they whisper.
En: Into what misery haue my Proiects flung me?
they shanot know I vnderstand 'em, that.
I
I were quitt with loss of both my eares, although [FOL. 72b]
I cut my haire, like a Lay Elder too,
to shew the naked Conyholes, I doe thinke
what cursed Balletts will be made vpon me,
and sung to diuilish tunes, at faire, and Marketts,
to call in Cutpurses. In a puppet play
were but my storie written by some scholler,
twould put downe hocas pocas, and the tumblers
and draw more audience, then the Motion
of Niniuie or the dainty docile horse,
that snorts at Spaine, by an instinct of Nature.
Ca: Ile leaue him to you, and seeke out Captaine Vnderwit
\S^{r}/ Ri: Come Master Engine weele to horse imediately.
Enter Courtwell, Sister and Deuice
Co: So we are fast enough, and now I haue thee
ile tell thee all the fault I find, thou hast
a litle too much witt to bee a wife.
it
it could not be too nimble for a Mistresse; [FOL. 73a]
Deuice, there is a part still of your pennance
behind, you would pretend to be a Poet,
ile not disgrace the name, to call thee one,
but let me haue rimes against we go to bed
two Anagrams that weigh an ounce, with coment;
and after that in verse your Affidauit,
that you doe wish vs ioy, and I discharge you.

2519 *counterfeits,*] ,* 2525 *cut*] *u* first minim retraced 2527 *cursed*] *d* altered *Balletts*] *a* upper loop not closed
2528 *sung*] *u* altered* from *i* *tunes,*] ,* *Marketts,*] ,* 2529 *Cutpurses*] *rs* misformed 2530 *scholler,*] ,*
2532 *audience,*] ,* 2534 *Nature.*] .* 2536 *S^{r}*] interlined above *Ri:* *imediately.*] .* 2542 *Deuice,*] ,*
2544 *thee*] ^{2}*e* altered *one,*] ,* 2548 *you.*] .*

De. tis tyme I were at study then –
Co: about 'em, your double congey, and depart with silence.
Now prethe tell me, who reported I
had wrong'd a Ladie, wast not thy reuenge
to make me angrie?
Sis. 'twas, indeed, now tell me
why at the first approach, seem'd you so
modest
[Co]: you haue confidence to spare now
troth
Co. troth I came not [Fol. 73b]
with any wooing purpose, onely to please
my Vncle, and try thy witt, and that conuerted me
Enter Thomas.
Tho: did you see my Master Captaine Vnderwitt?
Co: yes, hee's talking with the Priest, and M:ris Dorothy,
Tho: her fathers footman was here, she is a knights daughter
and heire, but she does not know it yet,
Sis. I thinke so
Co: wheres my Vncle?
Tho. a mile ons way to London by this tyme wth Sr. Richard, I long
to see my Master Exit
Co: wee shall want companie to dance.
Enter Ladie
Sis. My Sister.
Co: If you please Madam, you may call me Brother
we haue been at, I Iohn take the Elizabeth.
a Possett and foure naked thighes abed, [Fol. 74a]
tonight, will bid faire earnest for a boy too.
Sis. tis euen so Madam, the Preist has done it.
La: May then all ioyes attend you, if this had
been knowne, it might haue staid Sir Richard, and
your Vncle one day more.
Enter Vnderwit Dorothy Captaine Thomas.
Vn. Come for an other Couple,
Tho. in hell, my Master is married,

2550 *silence*] [1]*e* altered from *n* 2557 *[Co]*] deleted, probably Hand 1 2558] added* *Co.*] *C* top flourished 2565 *yet,*] ,* 2568 *a*] right-hand downstroke retraced* 2570 *dance.*] .* 2574 *at,*] ,* 2575 *abed,*] ,* 2576 *too,*] , , * preceded by Hand 1 . 2580 *more.*] .*, preceded by Hand 1 . 2582 *Couple,*] ,* 2583 *married,*] ,*

la. My husband left some Letters, and a token
was sent you M[ris]. Dorothy, you did ill
to obscure your selfe so much. you shall not want
hereafter all respects, that may become you,
Do: Madam I know not what you meane,
Cap: She wonot take it vpon her yet,
Vn. theres the sport.

Enter Device.

De: Oh Madam newes, ill newes, an accident – [FOL. 74b]
will blast all your mirth, Sir Francis –
Ca: La: what of him – ?
De has brooke –
Ca: his neck?
De. you guest very neere it, but his Shoulder
has sau'd that ioynt, a fall from's horse they say,
hath much endanger'd him
Co: My Vncle hurt – exit
la. he has kept his word, now if he but counterfeit handsomly,
Vn. Mounsier Deuice, I must entreat a Courtesie,
you haue wit, and I [will] \would/ haue a Masque
to entertaine my new fatherinlaw S[r]. Walter
Litleland, Mistres Dorothy, now my wife, is
his onely Daughter and heire,
Do. who has guld you thus. I am no knights Daughter.
you may spare your poeticall inuention sir
De. giue you ioy Captaine. [FOL. 75a]
Vn. she is still loth to confesse it,

Enter S[r]. Francis, Lady. Courtwell, Sister Captaine.

Fr. if you haue Charity a bone setter –
la. he does counterfeit rarely, wheres S[r]. Richard?
Fr: he rid before, but I sent my footman to tell him
this misfortune, oh Madam.
La. this is better then the toothach, he carries it excellently,
Fr: ask me no torturing questions, I desire
Madam a litle conference with you,

2586 *much.*] .* 2587 *respects,*] ,* *that*] *h* blotted 2594 *Ca:*] *a* altered from *o* *La:*] *:* misformed 2601 *word,*] ,* *handsomly,*] ,* 2603 *[will]*] single-stroke deletion * *would*] interlined above deletion* 2616 *is*] *i* altered from *i*

ile thanke the rest, if they withdraw, oh
letts leaue him
Vn. wee'le to my Chamber Captaine
Cap. you haue a mind to examine the busines priuatly –
Do. No good Captaine you may be present. ext
Ca: Come Thomas, thou shat be witnes too,
la: they are gone. they feigne most artificially, [FOL. 75b]
Let me embrace you.
Fr: Oh! take heed,
la: what's the matter?
Fr: tis no dissembling Madam, I haue had
a fall indeed, a dreadfull fall, I feele it
I thinke my horse saw the Diuell in some hedg,
ere I had rid three furlongs, gaue a start,
pitcht me of ons back like a barr, and broke
a flint with my shoulder I thinke, w^{c}h stroke fire too,
there was something like it, in my eyes, Ime punish'd –
la: but is this serious are you hurt indeed?
Fr: hurt? I ha broke my Shoulder feelingly,
and I am of opinion, when I doe
enioy you Madam I shall breake my neck,
that will be next, Ile take this for a warning
and will leaue of in tyme.
La: this makes me tremble, [FOL. 76a]
Fr. I will be honest now, and so forgiue me,
not the Surgeon come yet?
La. heauen hath cur'd vs both,
Fr. I am not cured yet, oh for the bone setter.
if ere I counterfeit agen.
la: there is a blessing falne vpon my blood
your only charme had power to make my thoughts
wicked, and your conversion disinchants me,
may both our liues be such, as heauen may not
grieue to haue shew'd this bounty.
Enter Courtwell.

2619 *the*] secretary *e* altered from italic *ee* 2625 *gone.*] .* 2626 *you.*] .* 2627 *Oh!*] !*, preceded by Hand 1 , 2637 *feelingly,*] ,* 2639 *neck,*] ,* 2642 *tremble,*] ,*, preceded by Hand 1 , 2650 *wicked,*] ,* *me,*] ,* 2652 *bounty.*] .*

Co: S^{r}: Richard Madam.
la. you may enter now sir.

Enter the rest and Sir Richard.

Ri: I do not like this stratageme, S^{r}. Francis
must not heere practise his Court trickes I wo'not

Enter Surgeon [Fol. 76b]

trust my wiues Surgerie, hee's come, how ist
noble Sr Francis? best withdraw, ile see
him drest my selfe.

they lead out S^{r}. Francis

Enter Vnderwit, Dorothy Captaine, Thomas

Vn. Madam and gentlemen M^{ris}. Dorothy wo'not acknowledge
she is a knights Daughter, she sweares she knowes no \Litleland/
Do [Litleland] till it appeare to whome this gemme was meant,
deare Madam be you treasurer, I confesse
I haue wealth enough, in such a noble husband –
la: it shall belong to thee, be honest Dorothy.
and vse him well.
Do. with my best study Madam.
Ca. where is the footman you talke of?
Tho. he pretended Letters to carry two mile of to a kinsman,
of his Masters, and returne presently, he dranke
three or fower beere glasses of Sack,
and he ran away so lightlie
Do: his reward shall ouertake him.
Vn: Will you haue her? she will do you seruice Captaine [Fol. 77a]
in a low Country Leaguer, or thou Thomas? ile
giue thee a Coppiehold.
Tho. You haue one life to come in that lease yet, I thank you,
I am free, and that's inheritance, for ought I know
she may serue vs both.
Ca. come, you may perswade her to looke high, and take it vpon her
for your credit, the gullery is yet within these walles
let your shame goe no farther, ye wench may prove right,
she may.

2654 *Madam.*] .* 2655 *sir.*] .* 2662 *selfe.*] .*, above Hand 1 : 2666 *Litleland*] interlined above caret 2667 *Do*] added, Hand 1 *[Litleland]*] single-stroke deletion, probably Hand 1 2668 *deare*] ^{1}*e* retraced 2671 *well.*] .* 2674 *Tho.*] *o* has open top *kinsman,*] ,* 2675 *returne*] blot beneath ^{2}*e* 2676 *Sack,*] ,*, preceded by Hand 1 , 2678 *him.*] .* 2681 *Coppiehold.*] .*

Enter S^{r}. Richard. /

Ca. What news from Sir Francis?
Ri. Wife, I hartily aske thee forg⟨iu⟩enes, I had iealous thoughts \but/
all's right agen,
la. I will deserue your confidence.
Ri: No great danger, his blade bone dislocated,
the man has put euery thing in his right place
Vn: Dee heare Sir Richard, wee are married, [Fol. 77b]
Ri: tis well done, send you ioy, tis \to/ my mind,
Vn: Come hither Dorothy,
Cap: but where's M^{r}. Engine?
Ri. he rid before.
Cap. if the rascall haue any wit left, he will ride quite
away with himselfe, tis his best course to fly ouersea,
Tho. if he were sure to flie, he were sure to escape.
Cap: at the worst drowning is a most honourable
death then hanging
Do: My mother died I haue it by tradition,
so soone as I was borne, my father (but
no knight) is now i'th Indies a poore Merchant y^{t} brok for \20000.ł/
Ri: the shipps may come home. hee?
Do. you were best vse me well, now we are married,
I will be sworne you forc'd me to the Church,
and thrice compeld me there to say, I Dorothy
the Parsons [dea] oath and mine, for ought I know, [Fol. 78a]
may make it halfe a rape.
Ri: there is no remedy,
we can proue no conspiracie and because
I haue been gulld my selfe, gett her with child,
My Doe is barren, at birth of her first baby,
Ile giue her a hundred peeces.
Vn. that's somewhat yet, when charge comes on,
thy hand, a wife can be but a wife, it shall
cost me 500.ł but ile make thee a Ladie
in earnest.

2689 *Richard.* /] / very faint 2691 *forg⟨iu⟩enes*] ⟨*iu*⟩ lower portions obscured by damage *but*] interlined above caret 2692 *agen,*] ,*, preceding Hand 1 . 2693 *confidence.*] .*, preceding ,* 2694 *dislocated,*] ,* 2696 *married,*] ,* 2697 *to*] interlined* *mind,*] ,* 2698 *Dorothy,*] ,* 2703 *escape.*] .* 2706 *tradition,*] ,* 2707 *so*] *s* altered from ? *n* 2708 *20000.ł*] interlined above caret 2710 *well,*] ,* 2711 *me*] *e* altered *Church,*] ,* 2713 *[dea]*] single-stroke deletion; *a* right-hand downstroke incomplete 2714 *rape.*] . marked twice, Hand 1, preceded by ? Hand 1 2715 *remedy,*] ,*, preceded by Hand 1 , 2720 *Vn.*] . marked twice, Hand 1, above Hand 1 2723 *earnest.*] .*, preceding Hand 1 .

Enter Sir Francis and Surgeon.

Ri: how ist sir Francis?
Fr: My Surgeon sayes no danger, when you please,
I may venture Sir to London,
Ri: No hast now.
Co: Not tonight Sir, wee must haue reuells,
and you salute my Bride.
Vn. and mine. [Fol. 78b]
Tho. a knights Daughter and heire,
Fr: May all ioy thriue vpon your loues.
then you are cosend of your Mistres Mounsier?
De. but your Nephew knowes I haue met with my match,
some bodie has been put to the sword.
Ri. Come we loose tyme,
Fr: preserue your marriage faith, a full increase
of what you wish, confirme your happinesse

Exeunt.

Finis. /

2726 *Fr:*] : preceding .* 2729 *reuells,*] ,*, preceded by Hand 1 , 2730 *Bride.*] .* 2731 *mine.*] .* 2734 *Mounsier?*] ? point added* 2736 *sword.*] .* 2738 *increase*] *c* retraced